Praise

"In terms of genuine understanding of not only the craft, but the business, you won't get any better than Denise Simon."
—Judy Reyes, *Scrubs, Devious Maids*

"I am thrilled to have a helpful suggestion to give to the parents who approach me about their children. I know firsthand of Denise's kindness and talent, and think this book will be an invaluable tool in navigating an often difficult journey."
—Meg Simon, VP Casting, Warner Bros. Television

"Denise offers a wealth of invaluable information on the success stories – and pitfalls – that any child actor faces. Parents, take note! This is the book for anyone looking for help navigating the intricacies of a complex and often overwhelming industry while keeping their kids, and themselves, happy and whole."
—Rawaan Alkhatib, Editor in Chief, *Backstage*

"Denise Simon's experience and expertise combined with common sense and human kindness make this book invaluable to parents who want to know the truth about what it's like to have a child in the entertainment business."
—Tara Rubin, award-winning casting director,
    Tara Rubin Casting

"Denise has the unique ability to bring so many different perspectives to the table for young actors. She's not only a coach and teacher, she also has experience in other facets of the industry. *Parenting in the Spotlight* gives readers the full benefit of all of Denise's expertise and years of experience. This book is full of wise advice and insider information. I highly recommend it!"
—Pamela Fisher, VP, Abrams Artists Agency, Head of Youth and
    Young Adults

"My son is a young actor with a role in a television series. As a parent, there are so many things to learn about the industry. *Parenting in the Spotlight* showcases Denise Simon's many years of experience and her   child actors.

The advice and life lessons in this book are extremely helpful. This is a must-read for parents with a child performer."
— Karine Schnapp, mother of Noah Schnapp (*Stranger Things*)

"It is always gratifying to have another reference book for parents whose kids want to perform. There are never too many. This one also tells it like it is. Read it!"
— Nancy Carson, owner, Carson-Adler Agency, Inc.; author of *Raising a Star*

"Denise Simon gives parents a much needed introspection into the heart, world, and drive of the performing child. This unique passion requires unique parenting, and Denise's years spent working with youth in the entertainment industry supply the reader with an excellent opportunity for inside perspective."
— Konnie Kittrell, Associate Producer, Stagedoor Manor Performing Arts Training Center

"Denise Simon's *Parenting in the Spotlight* offers invaluable insights into the often daunting and sometimes overwhelming world of child actors. Denise's professional guidance has been instrumental in supporting my daughter's early career as a young actress; and this book is essential for anyone with a child who loves to perform. Denise tackles valuable issues such as dealing with rejection, balancing academics, resilience and anxiety, and important life lessons so that parents can best navigate the ins and outs of show business while still ensuring a nurturing and happy childhood for their young stars. This book is a great read for anyone interested in getting their children into show business. I only wish I had had this book to help guide me when my daughter got started in the business."
— Leslie Harrison, mother of Abigail Dylan Harrison (*The Affair, Showtime*)

"Denise Simon has written a comprehensive, smart, and practical guide for anyone interested in entering the entertainment industry. A must-read for any parent whose child wants to be an actor in this competitive field."
— Jean McDaniel Lickson, Director BFA Acting Program, Florida State University

"My daughter, Kristi Beckett, has been working with acting coach Denise Simon since she was 13, and she is now 16. Kristi immediately attended a workshop and the fun and hard work began. We live in Florida, so Kristi skypes with Denise weekly and attends workshops at least once a year. Denise has been a constant source of encouragement with her gentle style and hands-on approach. She has equipped Kristi with the acting skills necessary to successfully audition and land an amazing role with Nickelodeon. Kristi is on Nickelodeon because of Denise."
— Kim Beckett, mother of Kristi

"The most precious commodity you have is your child. When your child enters "the business," there are many advantages as well as pitfalls to be navigated. This book contains wisdom garnered over many years in the industry. When you read it, you'll have the power to help your child have a healthy outcome, whether they become a star or enjoy an acting experience for a short period of time."
— Jay H. Berk, Ph.D., clinical psychologist; past advisor, Screen Actors Guild Young Performers Committee

"Denise's book stands out because of her unique perspective as a talent manager, acting coach, and consultant, with over thirty years in the business working with children prepping for professional film, television, Broadway, and university auditions."
— Alan Simon, On Location Education

"Denise Simon is one of today's foremost experts on child acting. She has years of experience working with child actors and their parents, which makes the wisdom she shares in this book both practical and profound."
— Jean Fox, former owner of Fox-Albert Management, whose clients included Mira Sorvino, Scarlett Johansson, Jennifer Aniston, Zach Braff, Josh Charles, Timothy Olyphant, Lacey Chabert, Judy Reyes, Josh Hamilton, and Gabrielle Carteris

"Denise Simon's "Parenting in the Spotlight, How to Raise a Child Star without Screwing Them Up" is a must read for parents of aspiring actors! Informative and comprehensive, the book is

filled with practical information necessary not only to guide your child, but also protect your child's interests! Filled with wonderful anecdotes, it is a thorough, step by step guide to help your child in his journey to stardom!"
— Badiene Magaziner, M.M. and Faculty, The Juilliard School

"Denise Simon's advice is sound, and the lessons and advice she provides can last a lifetime, like being your authentic self and playing by the rules. She teaches professionalism, and she emphasizes the importance of relationships. In the end, the entertainment industry is people. Denise's book will help guide parents and young people on a path to achieving their goals, but not at the expense of anyone else achieving theirs. From a training program's perspective, young artists and parents who read this book and put its principles into practice will prepare effectively, connect in the audition room, and perform with integrity through every phase of their career."
— Catherine Weidner, Professor & Chair
    Department of Theatre Arts
    Ithaca College

"After four decades of training young singers for the needs of the Broadway stage, I've seen again and again how having a solid support network in place can help make a newcomer's career. My colleague Denise Simon has written an invaluable guidebook for parents, chock full of the same honest, frank, supportive advice she has used to mentor many, many successful careers through the often-daunting world of show business. In these chapters, you'll not only find specific, useful tips on how to navigate the casting process and deal with the ups and downs of the industry, but encounter insightful strategies for helping children to cope with rejection and learn to recognize what makes them unique and special. In other words, important life lessons for all children and adults!"
— Bob Marks, NYC Vocal Coach

Parenting in the Spotlight

How to raise a child star
without screwing them up

By Denise Simon

Author contact: denisesimoncoaching.com

Thomas Noble Books

Wilmington, DE

www.thomasnoblebooks.com

ISBN: 978-1-945586-03-3

Library of Congress Control Number: 2017906072

Printed in the United States of America

First Printing: 2017

Editing by Gwen Hoffnagle

Cover Design by Sarah Barrie of Cyanotype.ca

Dedicated to

My parents, who are my biggest fans.
My children, who have taught me the greatest life lessons.
My students and their parents, who are my best teachers.

Table of Contents

Foreword

In 1987 my former business partner, Adrienne Albert, and I wanted to expand our business. We managed child actors and we needed someone with a keen eye for innate talent and the ability to work with young actors. We also needed that someone to have industry experience and expertise. This is not an easy combination to find. We discovered Denise Simon directing at Stagedoor Manor Performing Arts Training Center, and knew she would be just the person we needed.

Denise has a magical way of helping kids learn to act authentically and honestly. She has a gift for speaking the same language as her young students, and beautifully communicates clearly and directly – instilling confidence and skill. During her years with Fox-Albert, Denise discovered many talented young actors, including Scarlett Johannson and Lacey Chabert, and together we managed others such as Mira Sorvino and Judy Reyes.

Through the years I've watched Denise blossom into one of today's foremost experts on child acting. She has years of experience working with child actors and their parents, which makes the wisdom she shares in this book both practical and profound.

Acting can be a tremendous experience for children and their families. The desire to be in show business as a child can help you in any walk of life. There are very few people who "make it" as actors, but having the interest, learning the craft, and getting in front of an audience is very beneficial for children. I have two daughters who were child actors and have seen firsthand how their acting experiences shaped them into confident, successful adults.

That's why I am so pleased that Denise has written this book. In it you'll find a wealth of life lessons that you can reinforce with your child so that he or she can become a successful, confident adult.

Read this book for its helpful and practical industry information as well as a myriad of ways in which you can support and guide your child to reap the greatest enjoyment and benefit from acting. It takes a special child to commit to the hard work and time required in this industry. Armed with the information in this book, you'll be able to nurture and support your child in an exciting and affirming endeavor.

Childhood can and should be the best years of a person's life. It can set you up for a successful adulthood. If the passion for performing is in your child, Denise's book will help you nurture it in a safe, exciting, and enjoyable way.

Jean Fox
Former owner of Fox-Albert Management, whose clients included Mira Sorvino, Scarlett Johansson, Jennifer Aniston, Zach Braff, Josh Charles, Timothy Olyphant, Lacey Chabert, Judy Reyes, Josh Hamilton and Gabrielle Carteris

Introduction

This book was thirty years in the making. In all my years of working with child actors and their parents I have been amazed at how many life lessons occur naturally during the process of working as a child actor. The clients and students I worked with during that time inspired me with their intelligence, love of learning, and commitment to being their personal best.

This book is for parents of children with dreams – children who love to perform, show an aptitude for entertaining, and crave the spotlight and the applause. If you have a son or daughter like that, you might worry that participating in the entertainment business will harm them. I found just the opposite to be true. My thirty years in this industry taught me that children who pursue their acting dreams reap great benefits from their experiences, whether or not they become adult actors.

In *Parenting in the Spotlight* you'll learn about the entertainment industry and how to help your child navigate it successfully. More important, you'll find scores of life lessons that you can reinforce to help your child grow into a successful and happy adult.

Your child has something special: talent, creativity, and drive. It is my wish that the information in this book nurtures those special gifts by helping your child perform. You and your entire family are about to embark on an unforgettable journey.

Master your craft. Empower yourself. Enjoy the journey!

Chapter 1

So Your Child Wants to Be a Star

*Without wonder and insight, acting is just a business.
With it, it becomes creation.*

— Bette Davis

At three years of age, Travis Greisler was singing the songs from *Cats, Les Miserables,* and *Phantom* from his car seat. A few years later he was staging shows at home by organizing the neighborhood kids and directing them in productions in his basement. He told his mother, Wendy Greisler, that he was going to be a director, but seeing as there weren't directing classes for six-year-olds, he decided he'd become an actor first so he'd be taken seriously.

Does this sound familiar?

If your child loves to act, imagine, dance, sing, and entertain, that creativity bubbles out of them constantly. Your child is the first to offer to tell a joke, sing a song, or get on the stage at summer camp. They delight in acting out all the parts of their favorite movies or they stage sword fights in the backyard, assigning roles to the participants. They dream of being on stage or in television or the movies.

This dream can be both thrilling and terrifying for parents. You worry that your child will fail and be devastated by rejection. At other times you worry they will be massively successful and spiral out of control, becoming one of those sad stories plastered on the front of tabloid magazines.

I have some good news for you. Acting and the performing arts are wonderful ways for children to explore creativity, gain self-confidence and life skills, and even improve their academic prowess.

How do I know this? I was one of those performing kids, and I spent the last thirty years helping children become performers. Some of my former clients have household names like Scarlett Johansson and Mira Sorvino. Others crafted productive careers as working actors on Broadway and in television, film, voice-overs, and commercials. Many others transferred the skills and life lessons they gleaned from performing into thriving careers in business, teaching, and education. I've seen the wealth of opportunities that performing can provide for children and families.

In this book I share the information and skills you need to be the very best parent for a child who wants to perform. Whether your child stars in a movie or a local community theater production, there are things you can to do foster and support them in pursuing their dreams of performing.

When your child is blessed with talent and a desire to act, sing, dance, and entertain, it's a gift. By educating yourself about the entertainment industry and learning from the best practices of successful parents, you'll be a wise and supportive guide for your child.

My Story

Acting is in my DNA. From an early age I'd create shows with my dolls and stuffed animals. I loved to perform. Singing and acting gave me more joy than anything else. My first role was

Mrs. Banks in *Mary Poppins* at age seven in summer camp. When my parents took me to an off-Broadway show, *Curley McDimple*, I just knew I wanted to act and sing for the rest of my life. I got involved in community theater, learned the guitar and starting teaching it at age thirteen, and won the Best Actress award when I was in high school. I went to the prestigious drama program at Florida State University where I earned my BFA Degree in Acting.

After graduation, I spent a year working at the Burt Reynolds Dinner Theater with such luminaries as Burt Reynolds, Charles Nelson Reilly, Dom DeLuise, Martin Sheen, Ned Beatty, and Charles Durning, among many others. I had the time of my life as an apprentice, doing laundry, scrubbing toilets, and serving as an understudy to actresses like Kirstie Alley. I earned my Actors' Equity card and then moved to New York to do whatever it took to become an actress.

Like many, I waited tables and went on many rounds of auditions. I worked in summer stock, regional productions, and children's theater. I also worked at summer camps for children, directing plays and leading acting workshops, including Stagedoor Manor, the premier performing arts training center for children and teens.

One summer a talent manager came to Stagedoor Manor and discovered me – not as an actress, but as someone who worked well with children. She recruited me into her company as a personal talent manager for child actors. I found my calling at Fox-Albert Management, where I developed and managed the careers of young actors. With my background in teaching and directing kids, I found this work natural and exciting. Our clients, including Jennifer Aniston, Josh Charles, Zach Braff and Timothy Olyphant, landed significant roles. My client roster included Judy Reyes from *Scrubs*, Scarlett Johansson, Academy Award winner Mira Sorvino, Lacey Chabert from *Party of Five*, and children in Broadway shows like *Les Miserables*, *Beauty and the Beast*, *Mary Poppins*, and *The Lion King*, among many others.

Today I coach young actors and their parents, provide preparation for college auditions, and work as an on-set child acting coach for television shows and commercials. I've been in the business long enough to be considered "The Kid Guru," and write a regular column for *Backstage* magazine.

I share this information with you not to brag, but to ease your mind. I've spent my entire career working in the entertainment industry with kids. I've seen the highs and lows, triumphs and challenges that families encounter in this industry. Now it's time for me to share my expertise with you, the parent of an aspiring star. I can't promise your child will become a household name, but I can promise your child will gain valuable life skills, confidence, and wonderful memories as they follow their dreams, especially if you gain an understanding of how this industry works and your role as the parent of a child actor.

A Real Success Story

I had the pleasure of working with Travis Greisler as he achieved his dream of becoming first a successful working actor and then a director. You'll read more about Travis later in this book. His mother, Wendy, was gracious enough to share her story for this book so that you can have a look inside what this family from Pennsylvania experienced.

When Travis couldn't find classes to take to become a young director, he drove his parents crazy to help him learn how to be an actor instead. His first role was in the chorus of a local production of *Jesus Christ Superstar*. After that production ended, many of the actors in the show gave Travis's parents phone numbers for agents and managers. Travis would come home every day after school asking if they'd called any – the closest one being a manager in Allentown, Pennsylvania.

After finally setting up what turned into a two-hour meeting, this manager told his parents Travis had "it," and started sending him to auditions. His third audition was for the *Christmas Spectacular* at Radio City Music Hall in New York City. Travis booked that show and only a few months later was cast as the understudy for Tommy at age ten in the original Broadway production of *The Who's Tommy*. Later that year he took over the role and his parents were able to figure out how to manage one child working on Broadway and another child, his younger sister Taryn, at home in Pennsylvania.

A year after *The Who's Tommy* closed on Broadway, Travis was invited to be part of the touring company of *Les Miserables*. Going on the road for six months was a little challenging for the family, but they decided that Wendy would travel with Travis and Scott would ensure that Taryn would be able to see her mom every three weeks or so. Travis and Wendy would go on to travel the country with other shows like the musical *Big*, and even around Europe with the singing group The Broadway Kids. They made sure to talk to their family back in Pennsylvania every day and spend time together regularly.

When I asked Wendy what advice she'd offer to other families with a child who wants to act, she said, "Just speaking from my experience alone, which is obviously all I can, being on the road with Travis was the time of our lives. We had so much fun. But I also had a husband who was totally encouraging. He said, 'Whenever you have your golden days off, go, do, see.' When we were in Arizona, we took a helicopter ride over the Grand Canyon. When we were in Seattle for six weeks, we went up to Vancouver and traveled around British Columbia." Today Travis is a director, just like he promised his mother at age six. He had a big dream, and his parents supported him in achieving it.

I share the Greislers' story to inspire you and help you see what is possible. You are lucky your child has a passion that gets them out of bed each day. So many kids flounder because they haven't found that "something special" that motivates them. Statistics show that most child actors don't end up pursuing acting as adults, but there are still countless benefits they can gain as they make the journey, including:

- **Self-confidence:** I have taught many shy introverts, as well as kids who were afraid to get up in front of others for fear they weren't pretty enough, talented enough, funny enough, or even smart enough. One of my former students, who is now the associate director of graduate studies and lecturer on physics at Harvard University, attributes his teaching success to his acting and improvisational training. Some of my former students pursued professional careers as actors while many others are successful in their chosen careers as chefs, journalists, teachers, business executives, theater company producers, and many other occupations. The one thing they all have in common is self-confidence.

- **Opportunities to pursue other careers in the entertainment industry:** Many of my colleagues in casting, management, teaching, producing, and directing were actors. We all studied theater in the hopes of the big acting career. At some point in my journey – in my late twenties to be exact, when I wanted more stability and financial security, I took the leap to the other side of the business. My acting training and love of theater enabled me to enjoy a happy and thriving career in the entertainment industry. My parents have no more regrets that I was a theater major; it now makes sense.

- **Pride:** Acting requires enormous effort and helps children realize their potential for success. When your child spends time practicing, cultivating, and perfecting a piece of art, they feel a great sense of accomplishment, which becomes even more rewarding when they perform in front of an audience. They carry that pride into other aspects of life because they developed confidence in their ability to achieve goals.

- **An outlet for creativity:** Acting provides children with a safe space for self-expression. There is no right or wrong. Actors discover things about themselves by working with their minds and bodies. If a child believes in their ability as an actor, it translates into a stronger performance.

As you can see, I am a firm believer in the benefits of helping children go for their dreams. If your child dreams of performing, you and your child can pursue those dreams no matter where you live. You don't have to live in New York or Los Angeles for your child to experience the joy of performing.

Anything is possible. By the time you finish *Parenting in the Spotlight* you'll have a clearer idea of what is required and how you can get started.

Chapter 2

Twelve Surprising Life Lessons from Acting

Goals on the road to achievement cannot be achieved without discipline and consistency.

— Denzel Washington

There are many books about the entertainment industry, how to act, and how to help your child land roles, many of them written by my friends and colleagues. I recommend you read as many books as you can to understand the ins and outs of the business. However, in my view it's paramount to start by considering the benefits your child will gain from acting. Being a child actor provides a fantastic foundation for success in any profession your child may want to pursue later in life. It's more than the applause and the opportunity to play a role. Acting can be incredibly beneficial for children who are drawn to it.

Whether they are on Broadway or in local productions, TV, or film, here's what your child (and you) can look forward to:

1. Following Their Dream and Passion

Acting is hard work. It demands time, talent, and constant learning. If your child is passionate about acting, they will have the experience of mixing that passion with hard work, a skill that will serve them all their life.

Because there are a limited number of roles available and many people auditioning for them, you can predict that your child will be passed over more often than they will win a role. It's just a numbers game. If your child is not passionate enough about acting to be willing to endure the rejection, they won't want to continue. And that's fine; that experience itself is a valuable lesson in self-knowledge. I tell students that their job is to audition well. If they get the role, it's just icing on the cake.

When a new student comes to me and says they want to act because they want to make money or be famous, I worry that they don't have the passion to sustain an acting career. The kids who make it in this business are those who are so passionate about playing roles or entertaining others that they don't feel like doing anything else.

Twelve-year-old Noah Schnapp and the cast of Netflix's *Stranger Things* won a Screen Actors Guild Award for Outstanding Performance by an Ensemble in a Drama Series. His previous credits include being the voice of Charlie Brown in Fox's *The Peanuts Movie*, and Steven Spielberg's film *Bridge of Spies*. His mother, Karine Schnapp, was kind enough to share some of the experiences she and her family have had with Noah's career thus far.

According to Karine, she feels that being the parent of a child actor is not unlike being the parent of a committed athlete. The child must really "want" it, and the desire cannot come from parents pushing the child into it. "Noah accidentally fell into acting by taking a local theater class with his twin sister, Chloe. While his sister did not enjoy it, he loved everything about the class. We exposed both our kids at a young age to theater, Broadway, and going to see movies with grown-up stories. This developed his desire and passion for it. It started out as a fun hobby. Today at twelve, almost thirteen, his attitude around acting is much more serious. He will lock himself up for hours in his room running lines, or reading a script. He watches himself on screen and notices what he could have done better. Never in a million years did I think we would find ourselves where we are."

Giving your child the opportunity to dream and taking concrete steps to make that dream a reality is a powerful gift.

2. Being Present in the Moment

Sanford Meisner, one of the greatest acting teachers of the twentieth century, defines acting as "living truthfully under imaginary circumstances." This is what I teach actors – to be present and in the moment. Learning how to be here, now, is an important lesson in life. Acting is really about listening and being honest. If your child is distracted – worrying about their audition, what will happen in the future if they get the role, or how their hair looks – they will not be able to be present and listen.

So much of our lives are wasted in worry about the future or regret about the past. Acting teaches children and parents to stay focused in the present moment, because things can change so rapidly: productions get delayed, scripts change, the lead has the flu and suddenly the understudy is going on stage. So many things are out of your control that it can feel like a MASH hospital.

Learning to stay calm and centered in a shifting environment is empowering for children and parents alike. A mother called me recently whose son was brand new to the business and up for a lead in a national tour. He was right for the part and had a strong shot at it. She was flipped out, saying, "If he gets it, we have to leave on tour next week. What's that going to look like? I have other kids." I had to tell her, "I understand that you will have to get your ducks in a row. But he hasn't gotten the part yet. To go there already trying to figure all that out will take the focus away from right now, when you need to help him relax, be ready, show up, and do his best."

Being present is not always an easy skill to master, but just imagine your child as an adult who can maintain their composure no matter what is going on around them. You can help your child learn this important life skill and perhaps gain more of it yourself.

3. Developing the Resilience to Manage Rejection

Rejection is a given in the entertainment industry. Most of the time it's not personal. Your child might not have the right hair color or height, or the director was crabby and just didn't like anyone that day. When your child becomes an actor, they will experience rejection frequently.

Experiencing rejection teaches children that rejection stings and is disappointing, but is not the end of the world. I teach my students that failure is their friend. It helps them learn to evaluate their actions to see if they could have been more prepared, and to accept that though they were not selected today, tomorrow will bring new opportunities. Life is not always fair or easy; the auditioning process teaches this clearly, which builds confidence. When your child learns that getting what they want takes effort and perseverance, they will become a more courageous and confident person.

Of course it's hard for a parent to see their child face rejection. It's very hard. You can be a great mentor for your child during times of rejection by listening, helping them stay optimistic about future opportunities, and helping them find the good in every outcome.

Karine Schnapp added, "Noah's natural personality is quite grounded, and pragmatic. This has allowed him not to get too upset by the disappointments. However, as he has matured, his competitive nature and desire to 'get' a role – especially one he loves – can sometimes trump the best attitude. Constant rejection is not easy for any individual – adult or child. The goal is to use the desire as a motivator, and recognize the audition is just another opportunity to practice, and always be well prepared. Once he walks out of an audition, Noah has developed the habit of ripping the sides in two and throwing them in the garbage. It's a mental cue that says, 'I've done my best, now I forget about it and move on.'"

4. Mastering Social Skills

This life lesson benefits every child. Acting requires many social skills including communication, collaboration, improvisation, professionalism, stress management, and confidence. Kids are just developing these skills, so no one expects them to be perfect. However, only actors with confidence get hired. Your child will develop confidence as they learn to step out of their comfort zone and try new things, whether on stage, in sports, or in the community. Confidence comes from knowing that you have skills and abilities. Each time your child masters a new acting skill, does well in an audition, or has a productive conversation with an agent or casting director, they gain more confidence.

Acting fosters social skills at every turn. Your child will experience many different personalities on stage or on set. They'll have the opportunity to learn how to ask for help, take direction, respond to feedback, and think on their feet when someone forgets a line or a prop goes missing. They'll continually be asked to try new things and they'll learn how to recover from disappointments. All these experiences will help your child develop maturity and confidence, which they will carry with them into adulthood. Later in the book you'll read interviews with former child actors. All of them mention confidence as one of the greatest benefits of performing.

5. Learning Public Speaking

Public speaking is one of the most common fears limiting adults. Making a wedding toast, presenting a business proposal, and speaking up at a PTA meeting all require the ability to communicate effectively and confidently in front of others. Performing will erase this fear for your child. They'll enter adulthood feeling comfortable speaking in any setting, which can lead to career success in many fields including business, teaching, public relations, politics, and the media.

Even better, you won't have to do much of anything to foster this life skill; it will evolve naturally as your child participates in acting classes, auditions, and productions.

6. Brain-Building

Acting requires memorization, reading fluently and with high comprehension, and often reading music. It also requires critical thinking, creativity, and problem-solving skills. All of these skills enhance academic performance. In 2005 the American Alliance for Theatre and Education found that "as compared with their peers with no arts coursework or involvement...students involved in drama performance scored an average of 65.5 points higher on the verbal component and 35.5 points higher in the math component of the SAT." The challenges of acting require children to work hard and be creative, which builds brain power.

Your child does not have to be a genius to act, but many children who participate in acting achieve academic success later in life. I remember working with *All My Children's* Eden Riegel and observing her academic potential. It was no surprise to me that she was accepted at Harvard.

All child actors in the US are required by law to continue their education. They have homework just like other kids, but have less time for study, which means they need to develop focus and time-management skills, which fosters effective planning skills. The Schnapp family are strong advocates for Noah's education, ensuring that he has great teachers on set and additional tutoring at home on the weekends. They want him not only to meet his academic standards but to excel. Karine added, "You never know what happens in the future. One day he is working, and the next day, it may all end. For us, higher education is a priority. College is non-negotiable. If he wants to do both at the same time, and has the luck of being able to take roles and some time off while in college, that is great." (You'll learn more about the educational requirements and how to navigate them in chapter 14.)

7. Growing Self-Discipline

Self-discipline is one of the most valuable life skills acting teaches. Being an actor demands a lot from a child. There must be time for homework, memorizing lines, acting classes, perhaps classes in singing or dance, auditions, rehearsals, performances, sports and fitness, friends, family, and for just being a kid on top of all that. All those demands require a child to be accountable, prioritize, set boundaries, say no, and reassess their priorities over time. For example, a child might focus heavily on auditioning in the spring and summer but say no to opportunities in the fall so they can play on their school soccer team. During the teen years they might want to decrease travel time so they can have a traditional high school experience, or they might want to get their GED so they can spend more time acting.

Child actors work in an adult business and are expected to be professional, show up on time, be prepared, have a good attitude, and work well with others. When they are young you will need to help them with time-management and self-discipline. However, as they age it is essential that they take more responsibility for themselves. When children have this opportunity, they develop the independence and self-discipline that will help them navigate the adult world successfully. They enter the adult workforce with maturity, a strong work ethic, and the ability to make wise choices. Just imagine the edge that provides!

8. Conquering Perfectionism

Our world teaches kids that they must be perfect, look a certain way, and compare themselves to others. Have you noticed that movies, television shows, and plays are full of quirky and interesting-looking people? Each child has a unique look and personality that will win them roles more easily than if they pretend they're something they're not. I remind my students that "to compare leads to despair."

When I was a teen actor, I tried to be someone I wasn't. I had thick, curly hair that I used to iron to try to match the other girls I thought were prettier than I was. All teens have that experience of trying to fit into the crowd. But in acting, your quirks and unique looks are assets, which means acting truthfully. A child can't learn to act truthfully if they are worried about their hair or a blemish on their chin. If a role requires skill in gymnastics, and your child can't turn a somersault, they'll learn that this opportunity wasn't for them, but that the next one might just be ideal.

Your child will also learn that it is okay to make mistakes. Everyone forgets a line, sings off key, or muffs an audition. Sometimes an error becomes the best part of an audition because it allows the director to assess how the child recovers and thinks on their feet. Directors know they are working with children who are still developing; perfection is not required. Personality and passion are.

9. Managing Expectations

Your child will learn that there are things they can control and others they can't. They can control how prepared they are, what food they eat, their physical fitness, and whether they get enough sleep or show up with bags under their eyes after a night of partying. They can't control if they will be selected for a particular role, how tall they become, or when their voice will change. Knowing the difference between what you can control and what you can't is a valuable life lesson with many applications in the adult world.

Another component of managing expectations is learning what is expected of you and speaking up if something makes you feel uncomfortable or is beyond your ability. If a role requires a

British dialect and your child is not proficient at that, they will not do well in that role. Some parts include profanity, which can be uncomfortable for many children. It is important for a child to learn how to communicate their abilities and needs clearly. This skill develops over time. You'll be asked to speak for your young child; however, as they grow older, give them the opportunity to speak for themselves and watch them grow more confident.

10. Gaining Exposure to the World

One of my students recently returned from a two-month touring production of *Annie*. This eight-year-old spent those two months in Asia, trying new foods, seeing a different culture, and having adventures that the average second-grader doesn't experience. Whether your child acts locally or on a world stage, they will meet fascinating people and encounter a diverse set of experiences that will expand their world-view and their understanding of other cultures.

11. Empathy and Emotional Intelligence

When your child assumes a role, they will learn to step into another person's shoes and experience their feelings. Great acting is fueled by the emotional connection between the actor and the character as well as the actor and the audience. Your child will naturally become more empathic and understanding of others' emotional experiences as they take on different parts. Daniel Goleman, author of several books on emotional intelligence, writes, "Our emotions play a major role in thought, decision making and individual success. Self-awareness, impulse control, persistence, motivation, empathy and social deftness are all qualities that mark people who excel: whose relationships flourish, who are stars in the workplace."

12. Transferable Skills

Regardless of what career your young actor decides to pursue in adulthood, the life lessons learned in acting transfer and enhance their professional success. Your child will naturally learn to tell a story, to think on their feet, to appear confident even when nervous, and to work collaboratively. Every one of the life lessons presented in this book help shape your child into a confident and successful adult, and transfer to any career pathway.

As you can see, there is more to acting than just the fun of being on stage. For children with a passion for it, acting provides enduring life lessons and wonderful memories. One of the most important things you can do to support your child is reinforce these life lessons. There will be many teachable moments in your child's acting career that will help them grow into a remarkable adult.

Because this is such an important part of parenting a young actor, you'll read about additional life lessons at the ends of the remaining chapters. These life lessons are for you to reinforce with your child. They are the keys to raising a child actor who is successful in the business and in life.

Chapter 3

The Passion Meter

Most actors really love it, that's what they want to do.
They burn to do it. And so they'll read a script and think,
that's an interesting part. And because they love acting,
that blinds them to the fact that the rest of it is pretentious
nonsense, which it very often is.

—Hugh Grant

When Pam Fisher saw *Annie* on Broadway, she was hooked. She grew up watching singing and dancing on the stage and wanted to be a part of it so much that she cried. Pam spent her summers performing at Stagedoor Manor theater camp in the Catskills and got a degree in musical theater. Her passion for performing defined and shaped her life from childhood onward.

Pam credits her parents for their strong support. She said, "My parents encouraged me to follow my dreams and though they did not have much money, they financially supported what singing, dancing, and acting lessons they could. I was very lucky to have their complete support."

After graduation, Pam spent a year performing on a cruise ship and then lived in Aruba doing musical theater. She returned to New York and eventually decided to open a youth theater training program with a friend. Today she resides in Los Angeles and is a vice president at Abrams Artists Agency where she heads the youth and young adult division. She is a developmental agent who finds and trains the next generation of breakout stars.

Pam's passion for acting provided her amazing experiences as a child actress and led to an influential career in the industry. She shared, "I learned about EVERYTHING that I am today from studying theater as a child; confidence, compassion, teamwork, and professionalism."

Pam has a unique perspective on this business as a child performer, adult actress, and agent who works with young actors and their parents. She's seen all sides of the entertainment industry. When I interviewed her, she recognized that being the parent of a performer can be tough. "Parents have to know how to be there, but how to also be invisible. To protect, yet somehow not get in the way. To support, but not pressure. It is a fine line. I'm always very impressed by the devotion of the parents of our clients," Pam said.

I asked her to share some words of advice for parents reading this book. These were her inspiring words: "We only get one chance at life. Find your joy. I am certain that every parent only wants their child to be happy. Support your son or daughter in all of their dreams. Being an agent was NOT my dream. I didn't even know that this job existed. However, being supported in my dreams helped to lead me to what I do today, and I LOVE my job. I wake up and go to work happy every single day. I LOVE what I do. Support your child's dream to be whatever it is that they love. It will lead them in the right direction and give them the tools to help them find their true path to happiness and success."

Passion Is the First Sign

If your child is passionate about acting, you know it. They're regularly performing around the house, to real or imaginary audiences. They're talking about movies and plays and asking how they can star in them. When there is a play at school or in the community, they're the first to volunteer for a "big part." They sparkle on stage or in front of a classroom, perhaps even getting into trouble for being the class clown. If there is a spotlight anywhere nearby, your child wants to be in it.

In my years of experience working with young actors, their passion for the craft of acting is unmistakable. Children with the dream choose acting because they have no other choice. It's in their blood, in their DNA. They act because they must. Nothing else satisfies them and fills them up the way getting on stage or in front of a camera does.

If your child is in a local theater group, trying out for the school play, looking at actors on TV and saying, "I want to do that! How do I do that?" then you know that they are passionate about acting.

Is That Passion Consistent?

Most children tell their parents, "I want to be on TV," or "I want to be an actor," at least once in their childhood, because, after all, acting seems like a fun game of make-believe. What child doesn't love that? However, acting is a challenging business that requires hard work and sacrifice. It's important to evaluate the consistency of your child's passion. Is it just a passing interest or something deeper?

When your child constantly talks about performing or wanting to be on a TV show or in movies, you can tell that they're very interested in acting. If they mention it once, or just in passing, their level of interest might not be sufficient to lead to success in the long term. As you're evaluating your child's level of interest in performing, don't just listen to what they're saying, but watch what they're doing. If your child is doing some of the following things, it might indicate that acting is their dream:

- Auditioning for the school play
- Trying out for community theater
- Making up skits and performing for friends and family

- Asking for additional opportunities to act and audition
- Asking for an agent
- Getting excited at the prospect of taking an acting class
- Searching for opportunities to act and bringing them to you, especially as a teenager

These indicate that your child's interest in acting isn't just a passing phase but a genuine interest and passion.

Does the Dream Belong to Your Child, Or to You?

Before investing in this business, be sure to ask yourself, "Whose dream is this? Is it mine or my child's?" When I was managing the careers of young performers I would sometimes see a parent dragging a child into the room – the child wasn't excited or even willing to be there. It is when your child pulls you to auditions or performances that you know the passion belongs to your child.

I've seen entire families uprooted from small towns and relocated to the "Big City" to fulfill a dream of performing that was the parent's dream, not the child's. Before you head down this path, check in with yourself and ask, "Am I one of those parents living out unfulfilled ambitions through my child?" It is a common theme in parenting, yet sometimes hard to admit. It's also not a new concept. Sigmund Freud and Carl Jung both noted that some parents see their children as opportunities to live out their dreams. We all want our kids to be happy and satisfied, but by pushing them in a certain direction we can hurt them rather than help them.

"Some parents see their children as extensions of themselves, rather than as separate people with their own hopes and dreams," said author Brad Bushman, a professor of psychology at Ohio State University, in a study published by the National Academy of Sciences. "These parents may be most likely to want their children to achieve the dreams that they have not achieved."

If you had dreams of becoming a professional performer and chose a different path, it is easy to want your child to experience what you missed. You know why performing didn't work out for you, and now that you have more life experience and the wisdom to guide their career, how could they fail? But the fundamental aspect of any successful career is passion. You might have enough passion for you and your child, but first and foremost your child needs to want a performing career for themselves.

Don't misunderstand me; sometimes our kids need a little pressure to succeed and to be the best they can. There is no problem with a few gentle nudges from you if it is their dream. Too much pressure, however, can also push them away. My daughter is an excellent singer, yet didn't audition for the school musicals or the *a cappella* singing group. My prodding did not help. As a matter of fact, the more I asked her to sing, the more she resisted it. Her resistance forced me to look at my motives. Was it my unfulfilled dream of pursuing a professional performing career, or just wanting her to succeed at something for which she had substantial potential? I know my daughter could thrive in the performing arts, yet that is not where her real interests lie. I've learned to stop pushing her to do something she isn't interested in, regardless of her talent, and instead support her in her other endeavors.

Be Aware of Your Child's Need to Please You

As parents, we always want what's best for our child, and often our child wants the same for us. Your child can misread your support and encouragement as reflections of your own dreams for them. To please you, your child might agree to go to auditions and attend acting classes even if it's not what they actually want. They don't want to disappoint you, let you down, or have you think any less of them.

Make it clear to your child that you want what's best for them, and that if their desire changes they have your full support in their other areas of interest.

Passion Is Not Enough

Show business is glamorous to the outside observer. It is exciting, exhilarating, and draws people who dream of living in that world into the footlights or studios from all walks. Insiders, however, know it is a lot of hard work and that not everyone is cut out for it. How can you tell if your child has what it takes to succeed? Look for these traits along with passion:

- **Talent:** It goes without saying that your child needs talent for acting as well as passion. Don't assume that if you get stopped in public by somebody telling you that your child has a right "look" for TV that your child should pursue acting. A "look" is fine, but if there's no passion or talent behind it, your child won't enjoy the process. There are many opportunities for your child to learn the craft of acting and performing via classes, camps, and experience in shows. Talent can be fostered and developed. But a spark of it must be present for it to grow.

- **Dedication:** Show business does not reward people who have a passing interest in performing. A child needs to be committed to learning, practicing, and developing their talent above all other interests. There is a lot of competition and many talented people vying for attention, so each child needs to work hard and drive their progress forward. This commitment means a child looks for opportunities to pursue their craft by getting involved in school productions and community theater. They ask for a manager or agent rather than waiting for someone else to suggest it. They memorize lines during their free time rather than playing Xbox or surfing the web. The mere thought of being late to acting class keeps them motivated to do their chores and homework on time. It's not a struggle to get them to focus and do the work needed to memorize their monologue or nail their dance routine, because they love it. The work gets done.

- **Resilience:** Everyone faces rejection in show business. While it takes some time to adjust to it, the experience of being told no is valuable. A performer can't quit when things become challenging. They have to go out the next day and try another audition. And another. No one is right for all roles, and there are countless reasons why one does or does not get cast. It is not personal. Understanding this is necessary to learning persistence. Courage, confidence, and resilience are needed every step of the way. Pursuing a career in the performing arts is a tough road. Talent and skill are necessary, but they are not enough. It takes hard work over an extended period to break through. There are many disappointments before every triumph, so your child needs to have faith that their work will pay off and that success is right through the next door you open.

Because you picked up this book, most likely your child has already expressed an interest in acting and you just want to support them in any way you can. Once you've determined that your child's interest in acting isn't just a passing phase, the next step is to take actions to support this dream. Your first step is to assess their talent and potential.

 Life Lessons = Success

- Your passion is important. Follow it for clues to your future.
- If you don't feel passion and excitement for something, check in to see if you are ready to move on to something else or just in need of a break.
- Natural talent needs to be fostered with experience and training so it can grow.
- If you really want something, you must dedicate time and effort to achieve it.
- Disappointments are part of life but don't mean you should give up.

Chapter 4

Professional Assessments

Love art in yourself, and not yourself in art.
— Konstantin Stanislavski

In 1992, when I was working as a personal talent manager for Fox-Albert Management, I opened an envelope containing the photo and resume of an adorable eight-year-old girl. There was something about her look. I set up a meeting with her and her mother.

When this little girl walked into the room, I was struck by her intelligence, her voice, and her serious desire to act. She'd already taken acting classes, had a professional portfolio, and seemed wise beyond her years. She was very verbal and driven. Her mother was organized and willing to do whatever it took to help her daughter succeed. I was delighted to sign her with our management firm and become her first manager.

That little girl was Scarlett Johansson. I didn't know at the time that she would become one of Hollywood's biggest actresses, but I knew she had something very special.

I spend a lot of my time assessing young actors and making recommendations. In this chapter I share some of the things that industry professionals look for when evaluating children at various ages, as well as information parents should understand about the assessment process.

It Starts at Home

Successful child actors are always performing. They love to entertain by singing, dancing, telling jokes, or staging plays with neighborhood children. You might get comments from teachers or relatives suggesting that your child should be in show business. When fifteen-year-old Broadway actress Hayley Feinstein was young, she sang in her stroller and strangers on the street stopped to remark on her talent. Hayley and her younger sister, Tori (Broadway's Matilda), loved to perform and would sing, dance, and read stories out loud at home, well before they became professional actresses.

If your child has a similar passion and talent for entertaining, you know it. Once you have identified that spark of talent and your child is asking you to help them become an actor, your next step is a professional evaluation.

It is important to select the appropriate person to assess your child. Look for someone with substantial industry experience, not only in acting, but as a talent manager, agent, or coach. Beware of scams. (See chapter 5 for information on scammers who prey on young entertainers and their families.)

You can easily get a professional assessment of your child's potential in any of the big cities like New York, Los Angeles, or Atlanta. It is also possible to get an assessment online. I offer Skype assessments and ongoing acting training to children who live all over the United States.

Many parents wonder if they must move to New York or Los Angeles to support their child's acting dreams. New York is certainly the center of the theater world, and Los Angeles for film and television production. Many films and television shows are also shot in Atlanta, Boston, New Orleans, and various other cities nationwide. You might need to live temporarily in a major city if your child is selected for a prominent role, but during the initial stages of their career, and certainly during the assessment stage, relocation is not necessary.

The entertainment industry needs child actors from all age groups. Turn on the television or visit Broadway these days and you'll see plenty of children. Here's what you can expect your child's acting career to look like at the different ages and stages of their youth:

- **Toddlers and tiaras:** Your baby is adorable, of course. You get stopped on the street and asked if you've ever considered putting them in the business. If your little one is personable and separates easily from you, and you are willing to do the schlepping, go for it. As an infant, they won't remember the rejection. You don't have to spend money on classes or professional photos; snapshots work fine at this age, as they are growing and changing daily; and classes for babies – seriously? I don't like to turn down work, but when asked to coach a two-year-old, I must say no. Find a mommy-and-me class. At this age, let them play.

- **Early readers:** Children age five to seven are just grasping the concept of reading, so encourage reading out loud to further this skill for your young actor – but make sure they're exploring their imagination and having fun. An improvisation class or game-inspired acting class is the way to go at this age, while being careful not to over-coach. If your child likes to sing, encourage them. According to vocal teacher Monica Robinson, most vocal coaches do not start training until the student is about age eight, when their attention span can allow them to learn good vocal habits. If they audition for musical theater, it is wise to check in with a professional vocal coach and get their assessment. There are plenty of audition opportunities for adorable, charismatic kids this age – just make sure your child enjoys the process.

- **Primetime players:** Agents and managers love when I recommend actors age eight to eleven. Their voice is unchanged, they're disciplined enough for long work hours, they're reading, they're not old enough to have developed acne, and they're still the height of a child. There are many roles for kids this age in all mediums, and agents and managers are hungry to represent them, especially if they are not only cute but can act!

- **The awkward teen years:** Braces, acne, budding breasts – your little girl is no longer a child. She is now a young woman and in the throes of adolescence. She can start doubting herself as she is separating from Mom and Dad, lacking the confidence she once had. Roles are scarce in professional theater; she's too tall to play a kid, but not old enough to handle the maturity and skill some roles require. There is still plenty of work in commercials, TV, and film. Your child should get experience working in student films and start to build a demo reel of their on-camera experience. Real teens are needed – not adults playing teens – so be prepared when the opportunity strikes. Now is a great time for them to take classes and master skills beyond their natural ability.

- **Not quite an adult:** At sixteen or seventeen, your young man is now driving. He doesn't need Mom to take him to auditions anymore, but he still needs a tutor, and there are working restrictions on set. There are plenty of eighteen-year-olds who can play someone younger, and it won't cost the production company money for tutoring. If your teenaged son wants to further his acting career, this is a very good time to study and prepare for college theater auditions, as getting into a good program is more competitive than ever.

Whatever your child's age, there are always opportunities for work in show business. Just make sure the passion is coming from them, not you. You are their greatest advocate, and with your support and a small nudge now and then, you will have a very happy child.

The Assessment Process

When a parent tells me they want to know if their child has what it takes and if they should get into the business, I assess several areas:

1. Skills

First I ask about the child's interests. There are some kids who love musical theater and aspire to be on Broadway. Looking at them in that respect, I'm going to need to hear them sing. I might ask to see some video footage of performing they've done to evaluate their stage presence. I listen for vocal proficiency and vocal damage, and of course assess the acting of their song to see if they can tell the story.

In many cases I give them material to prepare for me just as if they were auditioning for a potential agent or manager. I give them material in all areas to see where their strengths and weaknesses lie. I ask most kids to read a script for a commercial just to see how they do with a simple piece of copy for which they don't have to play a character. I review their film footage, if they have any, to see how they look and act on camera. Sometimes I ask them to prepare a monologue to see how they approach memorized material and character development. And I always give them a scene from theater, TV, or film to prepare to assess their acting and listening skills.

2. Attention Span, Listening Skill, and the Ability to Relate to Adults and Take Direction

I ask the child many questions during the assessment to see how they connect with me. I'm looking for authenticity and charisma. It's understandable if they are a little nervous at the beginning, but I want to see if they can relax and speak confidently with a new adult, as well as follow simple instructions.

Listening is one of the most critical skills in acting. Your child must listen to the director, fellow cast members, and many other adults while auditioning and rehearsing. This type of listening requires focus. If they are easily distracted and cannot maintain focus, it will be difficult for them to succeed in the entertainment industry.

3. Type

Type is a combination of sex; age; vocal sound; physical traits such as race, height, body type, and coloring; and personality traits. Some examples of *types* that young performers play are:

- The cool kid
- Nerdy or awkward
- The popular girl who gets the guy
- Football jock
- Bully
- Quirky or comedic sidekick
- Chubby or overweight boy or girl
- The villain

Once an actor is established (aka famous), they can play *against type*. But while young and gaining experience, your child is most likely going to play who they are rather than against type. Getting a general idea of your child's type helps you both gravitate toward auditions and opportunities that best fit their type. However, it is wise to audition for roles outside of type in case your child's audition changes the mind of the casting director.

If your child has a disability, it is still possible for them to be an actor. There is a place for everyone in the business, but be aware that opportunities for a disabled child aren't as easy to find. Your job is to continue to encourage your child's dream and to give them all the tools you can for success.

4. Marketability

The good news is that there's a place for everybody. Just turn on the TV and you'll see actors in every shape and size. In today's market:

- Boys work more than girls.
- Ethnically diverse actors are in higher demand than ever.
- If your child can play someone who is younger than their age, you're in luck.

To improve your child's marketability:

- Develop their humor. Comedy is hard. If you child is naturally funny, that's a big plus. Help them develop their comedic timing through training in or practicing improvisation and observing human behavior and others' reactions and approaches to comedy.
- Encourage your child to be real and be themselves, with all their quirks and uniqueness.
- Have your child practice speaking clearly with no dialect.
- Develop your child's special skills. Any skill they can put in their back pocket is a huge help. Playing a musical instrument is a huge plus. Special skills can be:
  - Playing an instrument
  - Singing
  - Dancing
  - Speaking in accents
  - Acrobatics
  - Speaking another language

Talent can always be improved. I use this analogy with the children I work with: If I handed you a violin and told you to play, you'd tell me that you couldn't because you've never learned. Acting is the same. It's more than reading well; it's a skill that can be learned, practiced, and honed.

Some children just have a natural ability for standing up in front of people and telling or reading a story while their personality shines. But just like learning to play the violin, this skill can only improve with lessons and practice. Everything can be taught if the passion is there. I love to dance; but that doesn't mean that I'm a great dancer. But I can improve. It's the same with your child – skills can be taught, while passion and willingness to learn will carry them a long way.

5. The "It Factor": Star Quality

This trait is hard to define but easy to spot. I can usually tell if a child has the "it factor" as soon as they walk into the room and begin speaking. It's a combination of charisma, confidence, excitement, and wisdom that makes the child engaging, real, and fun to watch. Industry professionals can spot this star quality quickly.

6. Emotional Stability

A teenaged girl who was raw and vulnerable came to me for an assessment. It was great that she was giving it a go, because actors need to portray vulnerability; but only when they're assuming a character, not when they're out of character. She was so overcome with emotion that she kept crying. She was frightened, wanted to impress, and wanted to do a good job, but didn't have confidence and didn't think she could do it. She clearly wasn't in a healthy frame of mind to be able to land a role.

Acting is not therapy. A child actor needs to be stable emotionally. We're asking a lot of them to be able to show up as a kid and handle an adult business, focusing for long hours, handling pressure, and being able to change things at the drop of a hat.

Preparing Your Child for an Assessment

If your child has professional headshots, a portfolio, video footage, and/or a resume, bring them to the assessment, but they are not required. A snapshot and a listing of experience and training, if any, will suffice. Don't worry about getting a particular outfit or hairstyle, and don't pressure your child to prepare for the assessment. It is important that they be relaxed and natural. Let them be themselves. What's important is that the real person shines through.

If your child has been asked to prepare a song or monologue, have them do that, but when I assess I want to know who the child is without their having done a lot of preparation. I want the child to review the script I give them, put some thought into it, and make choices about how they would approach it in an audition. But for the most part I want to know who the child is without their trying to be something else. Don't pressure your child to be perfect. It is important for them to be confident and well prepared, but not stressed and worried.

Preparing Yourself for an Assessment

I have seen parents dragging their children into assessments. This does not work! Your child must be passionate about wanting to act, and should drag you forward instead. Even if your child has talent, if the desire is not present, they will not do well.

Your role is to be honest, flexible, and willing to quietly watch your child perform without intervening. Being in the background can be difficult, especially if your child forgets the words to a song or becomes nervous. For this reason I have parents leave the room for assessments, as they can make the child feel nervous and judged. It is important to see how your child recovers from mistakes. Mistakes always happen, and they aren't a big deal. But the ability to move forward and recover from an error is a crucial skill for actors.

After the Assessment

Once I complete an assessment, I make recommendations about how best to proceed. If the child's skill level is not high enough to begin auditioning professionally or to land an agent or manager, I recommend classes and other skill-development work. Some children need to enhance their acting, singing, or dancing skills, while others need accent reduction with a speech coach. Some need guidance on their image, hairstyle, or clothing style. Others just need to mature. When a young actor demonstrates strong skills, I offer to make introductions to managers and agents.

Now that you know how professional assessments work, you can assess your child's potential yourself in an informed way. Go to www.denisesimoncoaching.com/readergift and download my free checklist to help you decide if your child is ready for a professional assessment.

 Life Lessons = Success

- Evaluations and assessments are part of life. Do your best and know you don't have to be perfect.
- It is always best to be your authentic self.
- Talent is a gift – one that you can develop.
- Trust feedback you get from someone with relevant expertise.
- Good listening skills help you in every part of your life.

Chapter 5

Understanding the Entertainment Industry

*I never called my work an "art." It's part of show business,
the business of building entertainment.*

—Walt Disney

Charles Hamilton's first acting role was in a commercial for Shake 'N Bake chicken coating mix when he was five years old. He and his mother moved to New York for his career, where he worked as an actor until age nineteen, when he became a professional musician. Charles credits his adult success to his early exposure to the entertainment industry. He learned survival skills and planning when he traveled the city with his mother for auditions – things like memorizing important numbers and addresses, how to be safe in any neighborhood, and to have emergency cash in your pocket.

He also learned to deal with criticism. He shared this story: "I auditioned for the role of Buckwheat in the film *The Little Rascals*. I'd gotten several callbacks. The reason why I didn't get the gig is because they said I didn't look ethnic enough. That got to me for a little bit, but it didn't stop me from going on auditions. Criticism can make you stronger and clearer on who you are and what you stand for."

Acting is an adult business. Actors are expected to have a strong work ethic, be responsible, communicate well, and manage their emotions. Allowances are made for child actors, but your child will be exposed to high expectations and demands. There will be times when they are asked to make sacrifices or try new things that are outside of their comfort zone. They will also learn about money management, taxes, and scheduling, especially as they age and take on more of the responsibility for their career. These life lessons will serve them well in whatever career they pursue as an adult.

It's important for parents to realize that working in theater or film is part of a business – a large industry governed by state and federal laws. The overarching goal of the entertainment industry is to be profitable. Yes, acting is an art; but lots of money is needed to provide an environment to support that art.

In this chapter you'll get a broad overview of the entertainment industry, the various roles played by experts, union requirements, and how you can spot scams. It can be very stressful and costly to be uniformed about how the business side of acting really works. This chapter helps you navigate the industry more effectively.

Professionals and Their Roles

Depending on the trajectory of your child's career, you will need a team of professionals. You'll learn how to assemble that team in chapter 7, but first it's important to understand the roles and responsibilities of each person on your child performer's team.

I list these professionals below in no particular order; some children begin in the business without an agent, with an agent but no manager, with a coach but no agent, etc. Once you review this list of potential professional team members, you'll be able to determine which ones your child needs now.

It is important to carefully vet any professional who will be working with your child before hiring them or signing a contract. First check their reputation. Start by looking at online reviews of the individual or agency. You might want to consult with the secretary of state or attorney general in your state to see if any complaints have been lodged. Reach out to other parents who can offer you tips, referrals, and warnings.

1. Entertainment attorney

Sally Gaglini is an entertainment attorney and the author of *Young Performers at Work: Child Star Survival Guide*. I highly recommend her book for in-depth information on the legal aspects of the entertainment industry. She graciously agreed to talk with me about entertainment law. In her opinion it is vital for parents to work with an experienced entertainment attorney before signing any contract. Parents and child actors encounter a variety of contracts, including ones with agents, managers, and employers. Each contract is governed by various state laws, so they can be complicated.

If your child is not yet earning income, you can still hire an entertainment attorney to review a contract. Never sign a contract without a review by an experienced attorney as well as doing your own research.

2. Agent

A talent agent (or agency) in New York or California is licensed by the state, and their job is to solicit employment for their clients. Most are franchised by the Actors' Equity Association (AEA) and the Screen Actors Guild – American Federation of Television and Radio Artists (SAG–AFTRA) unions, and are affiliated with the Association of Talent Agents (ATA) and/or the National Association of Talent Representatives (NATR). They are generally limited to taking a 10 percent commission for employment contracts, 5 percent for rehearsal weeks for most theatrical productions such as Broadway and national tours, and 5 percent for shows that pay $525 or less per week. Agents in other states are often not licensed and do not follow union regulations. They take anywhere from 10 to 20 percent commission on monies earned. Be sure to read the contract carefully before signing anything!

Some agents represent hundreds of clients. They use their eye for talent and industry contacts and resources to get an actor into an audition and secure a job. They also negotiate contracts. Actors are usually signed to a one-year contract and have a 90- or 120-day "out clause" if there is no bona fide work for ten days or if they didn't earn a certain amount of money in 90 or 120 days, subject to specific wording in the contract. Check the AEA and SAG–AFTRA websites under "contracts" for up to date information.

Some agents prefer an exclusive agreement initially. Others freelance, getting permission to submit a client by calling or emailing. They are testing the waters to see if your child is a good fit. You are under no legal obligation to work exclusively with that one agent, however you are still required to pay them their commission if your child gets a job. Ideally you want to be signed by an agent and know they are committed to you 100 percent.

Just as in many other businesses, agents come in all sizes with different specialties. Some handle only young performers, including babies; some adults only; and some both. There are even agents who represent animals. Bicoastal agents have offices on both coasts, usually in LA and New York. Large agencies can have different departments including beauty (modeling and print); commercials and voice-overs; and "legit," meaning TV, film, and theater. No matter how large or small, what is most important is that the agent believes in your child's talent and ability.

I spoke with a leading agent for kids and young adults, Nancy Carson of the Carson Adler Agency in New York about what parents should know about working with an agent: She shared, "Many people ask me to define the difference between an agent and a manager. Both, at their best, provide representation and support for young actors. You are generally safe in signing with an agent because they must be licensed and bonded. That entails a background check and fingerprinting, as well as supplying bank account and contract information. Agents also must be franchised by the unions they will be working under, generally Equity and SAG/AFTRA. Both those unions also investigate the agents before issuing a franchise."

3. Manager

While an agent's focus is to secure employment for an actor, a manager cultivates a career. They counsel, advise, and provide career direction and guidance. They generally have fewer clients than an agent, which enables them to give more personalized attention to their clients. A manager takes anywhere from a 10 to 20 percent commission on any monies earned, and usually offers a three-year contract with a two-year extension.

A good manager communicates with you effectively, helps you find reputable photographers; acting, voice, and dance teachers; and coaches, reviews your photo proofs, pushes for auditions, advises on wardrobe and general image, and introduces you to potential agents to round out the team. They also help your child (and you) manage success when they finally land that one job that catapults them into stardom.

There is nothing like having a manager who believes in your child, fights for them, and helps keep their spirits alive during inevitable slumps. A solid manager-talent relationship is absolutely priceless. Talent manager Lauren Singer, of Lauren Singer Talent, said, "Some clients soar right to the top; others take time. It is so rewarding when a client who you've invested in, who you adore both personally and professionally, succeeds. Managers are a support system for the family too. A good manager takes so much off the shoulders of an agent that they are less likely to drop a client who's in a 'slump' since it costs them little to keep them on. Agents appreciate managers because they can communicate and coordinate with another professional in the industry for a number of clients, which makes their jobs much easier. Actors with managers can be more appealing to agents, therefore more likely to gain and maintain representation."

As a personal talent manager, I coached and read with my clients before auditions (it helped that I am a trained teacher), and even taped them in my office, where we had the luxury of retaping until we were satisfied. On occasion I accompanied my clients to LA to screen test as well as letting them sleep on my floor when they felt down and out. I did a lot of handholding for both parents and kids, and encouraged them when times got tough.

Your child might not be able to get an agent initially, so a manager who believes in your child is a good place to start. They should believe in your child when no one else does, and help them get ready to garner interest from an agent. As your child enters the business, you will have a lot of questions and concerns. Unlike a busy agent working on getting your child (and many other kids) auditions, a manager has the time to offer support and guidance at the beginning of a professional career.

A manager can also be instrumental for an already working young performer. They actually shape careers because of the intimate nature of their job. Representing talent is much more than just booking a gig. Reading scripts, packaging deals, setting career goals, introducing clients to the right people, helping to get auditions, and working in tandem with both an agent and a publicist to help market a career as it grows are some of the ways in which a manager supports a successful young performer.

A manager is not licensed with the state and cannot directly procure employment for the actor. Instead of submitting your child for jobs themselves, they submit to agents who then submit to casting directors. This allows for a more personalized partnership, as your manager can select the right agent(s) for your child. This does not mean the manager does not get involved in the audition process. Many have good relationships with casting directors themselves and get on the phone to push for their client as well as get feedback after the audition is over. This important task of following up on the actor's audition can be critical, as it tells you and your young performer what to improve on to be successful. Often the actor did nothing negative in the audition, it was just that they weren't the right type. Isn't that also good to know?

A benefit of working with a manager is that while your child is signed with them your child can freelance with several agents, thereby having access to more auditions. However, freelancing isn't as popular as it used to be. Sometimes a manager holds off on getting an agent or putting a child in front of a casting director until they feel the child is ready.

Managers are not required to be licensed, so you need to be sure that the manager you are dealing with is reputable. Anyone can say they are a manager with no training or credentials. A manager can be a great addition to a young actor's career, but proceed with caution and read the fine print before signing a management contract.

One tip regarding agents and managers: You are generally not signing with an agent or manager, but with the company that employs them. The agent or manager can leave for another opportunity, in which case you're going to be contractually obligated to fulfill the terms of that contract with that company. Sally Gaglini advises, "If you have fallen head-over-heels in love with a particular agent or manager, you can negotiate a *key person clause*. This clause will essentially say that if your agent or manager leaves that company, your contract can end as well. Then you're not going to be bound to that particular company without your favorite agent or manager." (You'll read more about how to select an agent and manager in chapter 8.)

4. Acting teacher/coach

These are the roles I most enjoy. Acting teachers and coaches help young actors hone and polish their acting skills. They provide individual and group classes in a variety of acting techniques and help prepare for auditions and roles. They help young performers master the job expectations of a working actor including memorization; communication with directors, casting directors, and fellow actors; and how to handle themselves in a professional environment. Acting teachers and coaches support children in managing the stresses and complex emotions involved in being a kid and a working actor at the same time.

There is a distinction between the roles of coach and teacher. A teacher instructs and provides the "correct" way to do something. A coach partners and collaborates to help young actors find their own interpretation of the material.

Acting teachers and coaches are often brought in early in a child's career, and may be able to make connections with potential managers and agents. They are paid directly by the parent or child. Many of these relationships last many years, even until the child reaches adulthood.

There can be times in a young performer's career when the parent or child needs additional support and guidance from a certified life coach. Some of the things a life coach helps with are communication with agents and managers, stress management, clarity in decision-making, setting goals, and planning. I am both an acting coach and a certified life coach, so I can help with acting skills as well as personal development and stress management for both the child and parent.

5. CPA or tax advisor

Once a child begins working, it is important for a parent to consult with a financial advisor familiar with the entertainment industry. In some states like California, New York, Louisiana, and

New Mexico, the law dictates that 15 percent of a minor's gross earnings belongs to them and must be held in a blocked trust until they reach adulthood. This is called a Coogan account in California, named for the child star Jackie Coogan. Other states have different statutes and names for the required *blocked trust* accounts. There are also certain tax deductions a parent can take when their child is an actor. A qualified financial advisor is necessary when a child actor begins to bring in significant earnings.

6. Publicist

If your child has reached a high level of success and is starting to appear in the public eye, your manager or agent might suggest that you add a publicist to manage your child's media and public appearances. Public relations work is expensive, so it is not required until your child lands a major role. As when hiring any professional, do your research and ask your team for appropriate referrals.

Scams

Because parents seldom have personal experience in the entertainment industry, it can be easy to be taken in by scammers. Scammers are waiting behind the cover of some very legitimate-looking advertisements, web pages, business cards, and fliers. Don't fall prey to these unscrupulous hucksters. Be suspicious when an advertisement, web page, or person claiming to represent a casting company uses one of these questionable strategies to lure you in and take your money:

- **"I can make you a star."** Legitimate representatives and companies do not make grand promises of stardom, especially in the first or second meeting. Their websites also do not glamorize the life of an actor. Real representatives and companies know that acting is a tough business and that there are no guarantees, even when the actor is talented and has great looks.

- **"Earn up to $300 per day as an extra, no experience necessary."** If it sounds too good to be true, it probably is. Promises of high pay are red flags. According to the SAG-AFTRA Theatrical Wage Table, the rate for dues-paying members of SAG-AFTRA in 2016-17 is $162 per day. Non-union jobs typically pay much less.

- **"Don't stop believing."** "Chase your dreams," "Follow your heart," and other inspirational messages are meant to lure in people who are desperate for success and have little experience in the acting industry. Legitimate casting companies look for confident, successful, poised talent. Sure, they want actors with big dreams, but they don't specifically advertise for actors who are down and out.

- **"Rush" casting calls and "immediate" auditions:** Representatives in a rush are often trying to close a deal prematurely. They know that people tend to make poor decisions under pressure and are more likely to pay for a legitimate-sounding purpose. Legitimate companies occasionally cast at the last minute; however, they require you to submit a headshot and resume well before they invite you to an interview or audition.

- **Casting-call ads on Craigslist:** A recent Craigslist advertisement in the New York City area displayed the NBC logo and claimed to be casting for extras on a new TV series. Don't believe it! Established production companies in urban areas use established casting companies to provide extras for their upcoming shows. Those companies do not advertise on Craigslist, in classified ads, or through representatives stopping people in a shopping mall.

- **"All types, ages, and ethnicities wanted."** Specific roles require a specific look, age, ethnicity, or type. Be suspicious when almost anyone could fit into the advertised opportunity.

- **"Major casting company accepting calls until 10:00 PM."** If that's all you know, let it go! Major casting directors never hide their identity. Neither do they have operators standing by to take your call late into the night. Sketchy and suspect contact information is a big tip-off to a scam. Do not call agencies that provide a telephone number with no other identifying information.

What's a new actor to do, and whom should they trust? Before plunking down your hard-earned cash, follow the tips below and do a little research.

- Legitimate companies have legitimate websites. Try entering the website address at www.whoishostingthis.com. You'll be able to see when, where, and by whom the site was created.
- Search the individuals listed. If it is a successful casting company, you won't have any trouble linking the people behind the website to real people in the industry.
- Search the company name for complaints with reputable reporting agencies such as the Better Business Bureau, at www.bbb.org, and your state's division of consumer affairs.
- Be wary of comments on commercial websites, either positive or negative. Those comments, while sometimes helpful, are unverifiable and often misleading.

There are plenty of reputable casting companies working with real directors on exciting projects. Reputable casting directors accept new talent every day, often via internet portals, for a wide variety of projects.

Unions

One of the first questions I am often asked by parents is when their child should join the union. They often think the union is the ticket to booking jobs when their children get started in the industry.

It is a common misconception that union membership is a marker of success and guarantees representation or work.

The two main unions are:

- Actors' Equity Association (AEA)
- Screen Actors Guild – American Federation of Television and Radio Artists (SAG-AFTRA)

Actors' Equity Association (AEA) is the labor union that represents stage managers and stage actors. There are several ways to become eligible. You can join the Association by virtue of employment under an Equity contract. The initiation fee is currently $1,100, with basic dues of $118 per year. Another way to join is if you have been a paid-up member of an affiliated union for one year and have worked as a principal or "under-five" (under five spoken lines) contract or at least three days of extra work in that union's jurisdiction.

Affiliated unions include SAG-AFTRA, AGMA, and AGVA. The Equity Membership Candidate program (EMC) permits actors-in-training and stage managers-in-training to credit theatrical work in an Equity theater toward eventual membership in Equity. After securing a position at a participating theater, you can register as a candidate. The $100 registration fee is credited against any future initiation fee when you become eligible for membership. Eligibility under this program requires a total of fifty weeks of EMC work at participating theaters.

Equity permits a member who is under the age of fourteen to claim Juvenile Withdrawal status to temporarily withdraw from the Association in order to work without benefit of an Equity contract. An actor on Juvenile Withdrawal can later reinstate in the Association without limitation. Once a member turns fourteen, they may only appear in school or community theater with Equity's written consent.

For Actors' Equity Association rules and requirements, and for more information, visit www.actorsequity.org.

SAG-AFTRA: Children working in film, television, new media, or other recorded media are eligible to join SAG-AFTRA and be protected by the largest entertainment union in the world. Children younger than four are permitted to work under SAG-AFTRA union contracts without joining. SAG-AFTRA does its utmost to protect a young performer's safety and wages; however, it is always the parent or guardian's responsibility to insure that children are being treated fairly and with respect.

Joining SAG-AFTRA is dependent on providing proof of appropriate employment, either in a principal role or in three union-covered background roles. Another way to join is if the performer has been a paid-up member of an affiliated union for one year and has worked as a principal in that union's jurisdiction. Affiliated unions include AEA, ACTRA, AGMA, and AGVA. More detailed information can be obtained by speaking with the union's membership department. General information including a list of membership benefits, how to qualify, and what SAG-AFTRA does can be found on the SAG-AFTRA website at www.sagaftra.org. Parents should familiarize themselves with the various contract protections, applicable state laws, and trust accounts (sometimes referred to as Coogan accounts) created specifically for young performers.

As of March 2017, the national initiation fee for SAG-AFTRA is $3,000, and the annual membership dues are a few hundred dollars plus 1.575 percent of all individual earnings under SAG-AFTRA contracts between $1 and $500,000.

Unions have been protecting actors and securing jobs for over eighty years, and their work is not to be underappreciated. Should your child land large roles or become a regularly employed actor, joining the union is a requirement. Union membership provides some necessary safeguards for child actors, including parental or guardian supervision, education, safety, compensation, and limits on working hours. The benefits also include pension and healthcare coverage, higher wages, residual payments, discounts, and access to educational and business seminars.

I don't advise joining the union until it is required. However, if you have representation it is best to check in with your team and get their opinion. Children can always be seen; it is a common myth that union membership is essential to getting seen by representation and getting auditions with casting directors. Membership in the union doesn't give your child preferential treatment in the eyes of agents or casting directors. The bottom line is industry professionals are interested in genuine talent and actors that will make their project a success.

Don't limit your child. Once your child joins the union, they are ineligible for non-union work. There is more non-union work than union work available to young performers. Gaining experience in all types of projects including student films, independent films, local and community theater, and even web series adds experience to a resume and provides learning opportunities in professional environments. When your child is starting out in the entertainment business, it's important to leave them open to all the opportunities available.

Taft-Hartley

Under the provisions of federal labor law (the Taft-Hartley Act), non-union actors who work as principals under a SAG-AFTRA contract have thirty days after the first day of SAG-AFTRA employment during which they may work any other job, union or non-union, before paying the joining fee. After the thirtieth day, the actor must pay the SAG-AFTRA initiation fee before working under a SAG-AFTRA contract again. For background performers, paying the SAG-AFTRA initiation fee after working on the specified number of SAG-AFTRA-covered positions is required before working again under a SAG-AFTRA contract, provided thirty days have elapsed since the third day of SAG-AFTRA employment.

Blocked Trust/Coogan Accounts

Blocked trust accounts are required in the states of California, New York, Louisiana, and New Mexico to protect money earned in childhood by ensuring that 15 percent of all wages earned by minors are placed in a special account called a blocked trust account and held until the child reaches adulthood. In California, these accounts are called Coogan accounts. New York calls their accounts UMTA or UGMA Compliant Trust accounts. Louisiana and New Mexico both refer to these accounts as blocked trust accounts but vary in the requirements for setting them up. Each state has specific requirements for these accounts. See www.sagaftra.org/content/coogan-law for additional information.

If your child needs a blocked trust account, start by consulting with your financial advisor and local banks. Not all banks offer blocked trust accounts for minors, and even some that do have employees who are not familiar with them. Explore several options to find an account with the best interest rate.

These national banks provide blocked trust/Coogan accounts:

- SAG-AFTRA Federal Credit Union
- Actors Federal Credit Union
- Bank of the West
- City National Bank
- First Entertainment Credit Union
- Morgan Stanley/Smith Barney
- Union Bank of California
- Wells Fargo

Each bank has different requirements for opening these accounts. Most require your child's name, social security number, certified birth certificate, and proof of your identity along with the initial deposit.

Once you have established a blocked trust account, ask the bank to immediately provide you with a letter, on letterhead, documenting these items:

- The name, full street address, and phone number of the financial institution branch where the account was opened
- The date the account was opened
- The type of the account specified as a blocked trust account
- The routing number and account number
- The signature of the financial representative who set up the account

As soon as you have this letter, make several copies. Store the original in a secure location. Provide copies to your child's agent and manager.

Work Permits

Minors working professionally are often required to obtain a work permit to ensure that their employment does not harm their health or education. State laws regarding work permits vary widely, so check with your state of residence and, if different, the state where your child is performing, to see what's required. Work permits are usually issued by a state's department of labor. If your child is from Ohio and working in a production in California, they need a California work permit.

In New York it is possible to get a one-time fifteen-day temporary work permit if your child is suddenly cast and has not previously been issued a work permit in the state of New York. In California, it is a one-time ten-day permit. However, I recommend that you apply for a work permit as soon as your child is ready to pursue professional roles, especially if they will be auditioning in New York or California. Most states issue an initial six-month work permit.

To get a child work permit you generally have to submit a birth certificate and documentation of satisfactory school attendance, school performance, and health, signed by a principal or school administrator. If a child is homeschooled, a parent can complete the educational form along with an affidavit from the school responsible for overseeing their child's educational program.

For more information on work permits, visit www.sagaftra. org/content/state-statutes.

 Life Lessons = Success

- School matters. If you don't have good grades, you will not be able to maintain your work permit.

- Laws are part of daily life. It is your responsibility to understand and comply with the laws of your state and profession.

- If something sounds too good to be true, don't rush in.

- Hire professionals to guide you, but do your own research as well.

- Working in an adult industry means you have to be responsible and have a good work ethic, even if you are a child.

Chapter 6

Acting Mediums: Stage, Film, and Television

If you're an actor, even a successful one, you're still waiting for the phone to ring.

—Kevin Bacon

Actress Lacey Chabert has done it all. She began as a young girl in beauty pageants in her native Mississippi. She later landed a role in *Les Miserables* on Broadway and toured with The Broadway Kids. When I became her manager, I helped her make the transition from stage acting to voice-over work, film, and television. She starred in the film *Mean Girls* and in the television series *A Party of Five* as well as doing voice-over work in *Family Guy* and *The Wild Thornberrys* while she was still a child actress. She learned to work in every acting medium: commercials, stage, voice-overs, film, and television. Today she continues her work as an adult actress in film, television, and voice-overs.

In this chapter you'll learn about the different environments in which child actors work and the specific skills required for each one. Some kids like Lacey can move between the various settings, while others concentrate on just one medium.

1. Theater

Working on stage requires a big presence and lots of energy. Children in musical theater are expected to sing and dance as well as act. The theater is a venue for performers to discover themselves. It is the only acting environment in which you perform something from start to finish; scenes are shot out of sequence in film and television.

Taking classes that focus on voice, movement, and acting technique is essential for children who aspire to work in theater. Theater offers the thrills and challenges of commanding a big space, though young performers must learn to command any space, no matter the size of the stage or audience. Musical theater requires lessons from acting, singing, and dance teachers. The young actor must tell a story in each song as well as hitting all the right notes.

Theater requires a significant time commitment from children and their parents. Broadway shows run eight times per week. Even though a role might be double cast, splitting the obligation between two different actors, the actors are still required to be at every performance. There are also rehearsals even after the show opens. Theatrical contracts are usually for a six-month minimum commitment. If your child is booked in a touring theater production, you and your child could be out of town for six to twelve months.

Most children's theater careers end at puberty and pick up again at age eighteen after puberty is complete. Many stage actors move from theater to other mediums during the teen years so they can continue working.

2. Television and Film

Television and film acting requires subtlety. Actions can't be too big or they will seem fake. Even a raised eyebrow is highlighted and emphasized by the camera. Children who work on camera must be photogenic. They don't need to be beautiful, but they must film well. You've heard the old saying "The camera loves him"? All actors have to consider whether or not the camera loves them to work in television or film.

Naturalness on camera is the most important aspect of film acting. Young actors have an advantage: the charisma that only a child can possess. It is essential to develop artistry through which they can let their personality shine without revealing their technique. The camera picks up everything the theater can hide, so mastering on-camera technique is essential to good film acting.

A young actor must learn how to convey their personality and presence on film. Knowing camera geography – their best angles and their physical relationships to other actors and the space itself – is a must. It is easy for the most talented young performers to freeze on camera and appear lifeless. The best remedy is constant exposure to and practice in front of a camera. Working in any film setting, including student films, is one way to gain experience on set. It is also helpful to take both acting technique and on-camera classes.

The skill sets for film and stage acting are so different that many university drama programs are now working in tandem with their film departments to train students to work on camera. This is a great innovation that opens many opportunities for graduates.

Television series have several types of roles for children:

- **Regulars:** characters who are part of the main fabric of the plot line such as the son or daughter of the lead
- **Guest stars:** characters who appear in one or two episodes
- **Recurring characters:** secondary characters who are featured from time to time in the story such as a neighbor, classmate, or team member of one of the regulars
- **Extras or background players**

The time commitment for a television series varies widely depending on the type of role. Many television shows are filmed in cities including Los Angeles, New York, Miami, and Atlanta. Movies are shot on location or in studios. A child's role could be just one day of work for a small part or a few months for a larger role.

The time commitment for working on a movie varies depending on the size of the role. It could be one day of work to several months.

Pilot Season

During pilot season, initial or standalone episodes of television series are filmed in hopes that a television network will purchase the series. Participating in pilot season can be a great opportunity to secure a long-term role in a television series; however, it's a nutty time of year when hordes of child and adult actors invade Southern California in the hopes of getting a big break. Traffic is crazy, managers and agents don't have time to breathe, and temporary housing becomes scarce. Although many television shows are cast throughout the year these days, pilot season, running roughly January through April, remains busy, with 100 to 150 broadcast and cable pilots cast and filmed. If your child is ready for it, here are a few tips for a successful pilot season experience:

- Schedule a team meeting with your child's agent and/or manager well in advance of pilot season to seek their advice. Both you and your child should participate in this meeting. Make sure your representative will actively promote your child if they decide to pursue auditions during the season. If your representative is on the East Coast, find out if they have a West Coast office to serve you. If your child does not have a manager or agent yet, I do not recommend participating in pilot season in the hopes of landing an agent there. Many agents are too busy to schedule meetings with new actors during pilot season.

- Choose East or West. Decide where you will be based. According to *FilmL.A.*, roughly half of the pilots made during the season are filmed in Los Angeles. New York comes in second, and is a viable option if you live on the East Coast. There are also a limited number of pilots produced in smaller cities, though the number is growing rapidly.

- Define your goals. There is no guarantee of landing a role in a pilot. It is a competitive business. Be prepared to consider pilot season a success if your child gains audition experience, new skills, and a better appreciation for the business of show biz. It is often the perspective and skills they develop early in their career that lead to success in the future.

- Put thought into relocating. Temporarily relocating for pilot season requires a significant financial and organizational commitment. It is necessary to secure temporary housing located conveniently enough to deal with last-minute callback auditions, and a rental car to navigate the traffic getting there. School-eligible children need to continue their education in a way that is acceptable to their local school if they are to work as an actor in either California or New York. Before relocating, it is also best to obtain the required state work permit and trust account for a child actor.

- Stay healthy. Both parents and child actors should exercise common sense, patience, good humor, and self-care. Maintain your good health and find effective ways to deal with stress. Without proper planning it's not easy to eat right or keep your sanity when dealing with traffic in an unfamiliar city while on your way to the third audition of the day.

- Sharpen acting skills. Don't wait until the day before auditions to have your child meet with their acting coach. Coaching helps them develop the best approach for different show formats, such as one-hour dramas, half-hour situation comedies, animated productions, Nickelodeon/Disney, and sketch comedy. For example, an actor should understand what the casting director wants when they call for "natural," "authentic," "broader," "quicker pacing," and "comedic timing." Young actors should enroll in workshops and ongoing classes in acting technique, on-camera work, and improvisation so they can handle whatever comes during pilot season auditions.

- Have the proper materials and equipment. Quality electronic and hardcopy headshots and resumes are required materials for any working actor. Have them ready before the season starts. Be prepared to submit video auditions with little notice. (See chapter 10 for tips on creating compelling tapes and video auditions.) Open a Hightail, We Transfer, or Dropbox account for submitting video files; most videos are too large to email. Don't post a video audition on your public website or YouTube channel unless it is password protected. Many projects are not meant to be viewed by the public in the preproduction stage. Violating that policy is likely to cost you the part.

- Look for other opportunities. Projects such as commercials, films, episodic television, voice-overs, and theater provide acting opportunities year-round. While seeking roles in pilots, look for these opportunities, too. They can provide valuable experience, exposure, and compensation.

- Remember that it's acceptable for kids to decline some opportunities. Pilot season is an incredible adventure, but it is also hard work. I advise young actors to follow through on every commitment they make and every callback they get. However, there are times when it is best to let an opportunity go and head to the zoo, Disneyland, or the beach instead. Avoid exhausting your child and schedule downtime with the same commitment you give to following through on acting opportunities.

Many young actors make the pilgrimage to Los Angeles for pilot season, but for reasons that are often completely unrelated to talent, few get substantial roles. With that in mind, I recommend that you focus on your child's readiness. Young actors who are truly ready can deal with the ups and downs of the business and still come out of pilot season with the same enthusiasm as when they entered it, regardless of the number of jobs booked.

3. Voice-Overs

With the rise in popularity of animated television shows and films, voice-over work can be a lucrative and fun way for child actors to work. There are even some opportunities to do voice-over work for video games, off-camera television, and radio spots.

As you might imagine, voice-over work requires outstanding vocal quality. Children must be able to read fluently and smoothly. If your child has a speech impediment or strong accent, they may need training to eliminate it unless the role they are auditioning for calls for a particular speech pattern, accent, or sound.

4. Commercials

Some young actors only pursue commercials. Even if they haven't had much training and don't yet have a lot of dramatic ability, they can land a role in a commercial if they have a special look, skill, personality, and/or quality.

To secure an agent for commercials, your child will be asked to read commercial copy. Ironically, when they audition they might not be asked to do anything but stand and smile or hold a prop like a tennis racket or a toy. They often don't have to learn many lines or go through a grueling audition process. It is usually one audition and a callback as opposed to many callbacks and screen tests.

There may be no diaglogue, just direction. The casting director is usually seeking a particular look or personality more than anything else. Your child might be told, "There's a cute boy over there who's flirting with you. I want to see what you do when he's flirting with you," or "Sip this soup and show me that you love it."

Training in improvisation is extremely useful for children who want to act in commercials. Improvisation helps you get out of your head, focus on the unusual, and live life truthfully. It helps you engage without thinking or second-guessing your choices, and act instinctually while maintaining your technique and confidence. It is a great tool for acting and for life.

Liz Lewis is a busy bi-coastal casting director. She shared, "Whether I am casting a commercial, film, or TV project, I'm looking for the child who is as natural as possible. Because a child who is good at improvisation will be much more comfortable in the audition, training in improv is a very good idea. It keeps a child from being too studied so that they can be natural. Improv training also helps them be more creative in the audition process, allowing the casting director, director, or producer to see how that child makes choices. When a child is natural and can make unique choices about the material, they have a better chance of getting roles."

5. Print Work

Print modeling is a great way to gain experience if your child is just beginning. Unlike runway modeling for which actors need to be a specific height and weight, print modeling needs real kids of all shapes and sizes. Working in this arena can teach a new actor how to be comfortable in front of the camera. Even though there is no copy to read, having special skills and even some acting background can help a young actor come alive and give the director or photographer just what they need. If your child is photogenic or has a unique look, print work can be a great place to begin.

6. Extra Work

Films, television shows, and commercials hire extras (aka background actors), and working as an extra can be a positive learning experience for young actors who are just starting out. Extra work provides a chance to work on a set and see what goes on behind and in front of the camera. However, it is not a launching pad to an acting career.

As you can see, there are different pathways for child actors. Some wish to stay in one acting medium as long as they continue to act. Others, like Lacey Chabert, move from setting to setting, developing the skills required to master each environment.

You and your child do not need to decide about acting mediums right away. Wait to see where opportunities arise. Consult with your team of industry professionals. The most important thing is for your child to follow their passion. Training in the required skills is available for every opportunity. Your child's interests and passions are the most important determinations for their acting pathway.

 Life Lessons = Success

- Life offers a variety of options. You get to choose!
- Change is positive and can propel you forward.
- When you aspire to a new goal, get the training and skills you need to set yourself up for success.
- Measure your efforts by how well you prepared and how you felt while you were performing, not on the outcome.
- When you do your best, you have won.

Chapter 7

Preparing Your Child to Enter the Business

If you risk nothing, then you risk everything.
—Geena Davis

Miles Thompson spent the last fifteen years of his life as a chef. Today he is the executive chef at Michael's Restaurant in Santa Monica, California. It's a high-stress environment with the need for daily creativity and improvisation. Miles credits much of his adult success to the skills he learned as a child actor!

Miles had a rocky introduction to acting. His first audition at age ten was for *The Lion King* on Broadway. It was crushing because Miles did a terrible job on that audition. He shared, "I had to sing. I had never been confident singing in public, and that was part of it. It just felt terrible. I remember being very upset afterward. But it was the perfect way to have your first audition being the worst one you ever remember because it just meant that you could only have better auditions from there in the future. If I had gone on the first audition and got hired, I probably wouldn't appreciate the process of auditioning and the process of being rejected as much. You must really understand that you're going to get rejected ninety-plus percent of the time. You don't hear anything most of the time. That has taught me a really wonderful lesson about just letting go."

Miles's experiences as a child actor are both inspirational and informative. Before we go over some of the specific tangible items your child needs to start their acting career, I want you to understand Miles's experiences, which highlight the mindset you and your child need in order to flourish in the entertainment industry. When you're prepared for the challenges you'll be able to help your child see the life lessons in those challenges and apply them to whatever career path they choose.

The ability to do your best and then let it go was something that Miles learned from auditioning early in his career. He always strove to be the best he could by preparing carefully and giving his all during auditions. Even when an audition went phenomenally well, Miles soon realized that he had no control over the decisions made by casting directors. He uses this knowledge to let things go in his restaurant as well. Miles can make the most amazing dishes, but he can't control whether or not patrons enjoy them. He learned to measure his success in acting by his level of preparation and how he felt about his performance, knowing that he'd get notes from the director after every performance on ways he could improve.

Miles shares a rather surprising benefit he got from acting: "Acting helped me in my romantic relationships. I'm a short, scrawny guy, not your typical leading man. When girls wouldn't go out with me, I just considered it like an audition that I didn't win. Romantic rejection did not wound me as deeply as it did for some of my friends. When I met my wife, it was easy, and I knew she was the one for me. Acting taught me that rejection was painful but normal. Life goes on, and other opportunities arise." Miles also learned that perfection does not exist, not in acting or in relationships. Instead he strives continually to improve his relationships, just as he did when he was acting.

Before your child starts auditioning, have a conversation with them about rejection. Share some of the things that you learn in this book so that they are aware that rejection often happens in this industry, and it's not personal or anything you can control. Your child will often not know why they were not chosen for a role. Talk about this before they begin auditioning and reinforce it throughout their acting career. According to Miles, "Sometimes parents think that they don't want their kids to be sad, or rejected too much. Growing up is the most chaotic emotional state you probably will ever be in. High school is going to be insane for anyone. If you are acting, you'll learn to cope with that teenage stress easier."

It's also important to prepare your child for hard work so they can continue to grow in their acting skills. Miles shared that working in acting classes helped him on many levels. At times he was the strongest actor in the class; other times he was the weakest. These experiences helped him measure his performance against his own personal best, not against what other people were doing. If your child truly loves acting, continuing to take classes and learn more skills will be fun as well as challenging.

Once you have prepared your child emotionally for the need to do their best and then let it go – to expect rejection, hard work, and the joy of continued growth, it's time to prepare some of the materials they need to get started. Here are six items needed to get started:

1. Headshots

Good headshots are essential for your child's career. A headshot is your child's business card. It provides a casting director's first impression, and in most cases it's a way for your performer to get their foot in the door. At first you need not pay a professional photographer; a good candid photo is sufficient for an initial interview. However, once your child starts auditioning regularly, a professional headshot is essential.

Headshots should be a natural representation of your child that shows off their personality. It should reflect what they look like on their best day. Don't try to create a costumed look or have your child wear clothing that makes them feel uncomfortable. Be sure the look is natural and age-appropriate, without heavy makeup or suggestive clothing. Have them dress in clean, nice clothes that make them feel good.

The days of black and white headshots are long gone, so help your young actor find the colors that work best with their hair and skin tones. Find something that makes your child's eyes pop – I recommend layering and textures.

Stay away from busy patterns. Don't style their hair in a dressy updo or pigtails if that is not how they normally wear their hair. No hats or accessories either. Jewelry can be distracting. Simple post or hoop earrings are fine for a girl. Skip the bangles and chunky bracelets and avoid necklaces. Remember that your child is still a child.

While cell-phone and point-and-shoot cameras are getting better and better, a professional photographer with experience in taking headshots of children for the acting industry can photograph your child in an authentic and flattering way. Finding a good photographer is one of the most important decisions you will make for your child's career. Get recommendations from industry professionals and other actors. Check out photos on the photographer's website or in their portfolio to see if you like their artistic style. Meet with or talk to them to make sure you and your child like them and feel relaxed with them. Do your research, choose wisely, and remember to be professional, courteous, and cooperative. This will help the photographer get the best shot they can. Ask these questions:

- How many shots do you take?
- Will you shoot until you get what you need?
- If I am not happy with the results, will you reshoot?
- Do you do the retouching?
- How many images will I get for the price of the shoot?

- Do you shoot in a studio, outdoors with natural lighting, or both?
- Will you help me choose the clothing?
- Do you provide a hair and makeup person for older children? Is this included in the fee?

Child photographer fees range roughly from $100 to $500 for the shoot and proofs. Remember that children grow fast and you will need new pictures regularly.

When you get the proofs back, consult with an industry professional to select the ones that will appeal best to casting directors, agents, and managers. Two photos are usually used, one with a smile and one with a more serious look to show contrast. An acting coach, agent, or manager can help you select the best shots.

2. Resume

A resume provides casting directors with your child's range of experience. While your young actor might not have much on their resume, it's still an important piece of the puzzle for obtaining work. It should not be just a list of acting credits, but also highlight their unique skills such as dance, dialects, and sports, as well as their training.

Design the resume in columns, making it easy to read. Unlike an adult's job resume, there's no need to include your home phone number or address; instead provide a cell phone number, an email address, and a website if applicable. There's also no need to mention your child's age or age range, because this is limiting. Do include union status and vital statistics such as height, weight, and hair and eye color. If your child is a singer, you can add their vocal type such as soprano, alto, or tenor.

For acting credits, include roles performed in school and camp plays, commercials, professional credits, local productions, etc. There is no need to include extra work unless that is the only experience they have. People in the industry know extra work is not acting work; it can give your child industry experience but not legitimacy regarding skill.

Be sure to list any training your child has had in acting, singing, and dancing, including where the training took place, how many years, and what type.

Skills to include:

- Sports played and the level of skill
- Instruments played and proficiency
- Languages spoken
- Dialects spoken

Don't forget other skills like skateboarding, juggling, magic, ice or roller skating, horseback riding, etc. However, if your child is not adept at a skill but just learning it, do not list it on their resume. If your child can drive and has a driver's license, this is also helpful information, especially for commercials. You can also add any special honors or awards won that are relevant to acting, training, or performing.

Keep the resume simple and to one page. There's no need to pad it or expand on it – no one expects your child to have extensive experience. And whatever you do, don't lie!

A headshot is 8" x 10", and a piece of paper is 8.5" x 11". Cut the resume to fit the back of the headshot. Staple the resume to the back of your child's headshot. This may seem trivial, but it is important that they do not get separated from each other. If they do, the beautiful picture of your child could end up floating around with no name or number!

Here is an example of a resume:

SUSAN WHITE
917-555-5555
susanwhite@email.com
SAG-AFTRA

Height: 61" Weight: 98 lbs. Eyes: Blue Hair: Blond

THEATER

The Sound of Music	Brigitta	Town Hall Theater
Little Women	Meg	Crossroads High School
The Secret Garden	Mary Lennox	The Little Playhouse
Brighton Beach Memoirs	Laurie	Actors Youth Theater

TELEVISION

Law and Order	Neighbor	NBC

FILM

Grace's Room	Grace	NYU Thesis film

COMMERCIALS/VOICE-OVERS

List upon request

TRAINING

Acting: Denise Simon Acting & Coaching, The Film Academy
Voice: John Jones, Melony Brown
Dance: Joe's Dance Studio – tap, ballet, hip hop, jazz

SPECIAL SKILLS

Speaks Spanish fluently, skateboarding, skiing, British and Irish dialects, piano, can tie a cherry knot on her tongue

Include a simple letter with the resume and photo. Here's an example:

Dear X,

My son, Brandon, is eleven years old and loves acting, singing, and dancing. He has appeared in numerous local productions, and we believe he is now ready for more professional work.

We live near New York City and are willing to travel in for auditions. We would love an opportunity to meet with you at your convenience.

Please feel free to contact me by email at sandra@mail.com or phone me at 345-555-5555.

Thank you for your consideration.

Sincerely,

Sandra Dee (mother of Brandon)

3. Training

Training is an essential element of your child's acting career. This is a competitive business in which luck, talent, and opportunity meet. Having the right look for a role is key, but talent is what wins out. A combination of weekly group classes, workshops, and private coaching is the best training regimen for your child's artistic growth. (This will be covered in detail in chapter 12.)

4. Audition Materials

Just as headshots are your child's business cards, audition materials such as monologues and songs are the portfolio. They should memorize two short, contrasting monologues that they feel comfortable performing for auditions and interviews. Choose pieces from published plays by good writers such as Neil Simon, Stephen Karam, and David Lindsay-Abaire. I am not a fan of generic monologues from monologue books unless your child is on the young side. There are plenty of monologue books with pieces young kids can relate to. A teen actor will make a much better impression with a good piece of literature.

If your child sings, they should also be ready to perform sixteen to thirty-two bars of a few contrasting songs. Well-known vocal instructor Bob Marks reminds his students that a *bar* is not a measure of time, and sixteen or thirty-two bars can vary a great deal in length. He said, "Logical sixteen- and thirty-two-bar cuts for singers should be prepared that maintain the integrity of the music, are playable at sight by an unfamiliar accompanist, show the vocal strengths of the performer, and make a coherent dramatic statement. A good audition cut of a song will sound like an entire piece, only shorter. It should tell a story or make a statement, and have a logical resolution." A ballad plus an up-tempo song and even a rock or pop piece is best. A personal connection to the monologue and song is an opportunity to show authenticity, skill, and range of diversity.

I collected a wide variety of audition materials over my thirty years in the business and often help with the selection process. Acting coaches and teachers can provide assistance in finding fresh and compelling audition materials, as can bookstores such as the Drama Book Shop in New York and Samuel French Bookstore in California.

5. Demo Reel/Footage

While a demo reel (or just "reel") is not essential for a beginning acting career, it can help. A demo reel provides images of your child and demonstrates their presence, how they look on film, and their acting ability. It's a bonus for casting directors, as they can gain a sense of your child's personality.

A demo reel, also known as a sizzle reel, is a compilation of an actor's work on film. It usually consists of twenty- to thirty-second clips totaling no more than one or two minutes. It should feature the actor in different scenes, starting with the most professional booking. Demo reels have opened doors for many actors. Like headshots, demo reels should be updated regularly. Children grow fast, and their looks can change. While I recommend putting the most professional and current scenes at the front of your reel, it's okay to retain dated pieces after those.

- **Material**. Clips from network television shows, feature films, independently produced films, and commercials are all desirable footage, but today actors can also include clips from student films. Universities invest heavily in professional equipment and thus give their students access to state of the art opportunities, but I have heard complaints from parents who were not able to obtain footage of their child's work. Make sure you draw up a simple contract stating you will be given a copy of the film or scene upon completion. Your child is working for no pay and should be guaranteed a copy of their work.

- If you don't have any professional footage, you can help your young performer put together something on their own using other good actors and good material. You and/or your child can even write something they connect with, but make sure you have good sound, lighting, and picture quality, and spend a few bucks on getting coached properly. A bad reel is worse than no reel at all! (See chapter 10 for tips on how to tape your child for demo reels and other purposes.)

- **Putting together your own reel.** If you have the footage and want to put the reel together on your own, be sure to start with your child's headshot with their name and contact information visible! You can also label the clip identifying what it is from. If you have a computer or know a handy teenager, they can help you work in iMovie or Windows Media Player.

- **Hiring a professional.** Another option, and one becoming more popular, is to hire a professional company. REELARC, a company specializing in custom demo reels, is one such company. They consult with an actor to learn their strengths, then write, produce, and edit a custom demo reel. The part is written for your child and highlights their strengths, allowing them to stretch their boundaries on film. The video is shot at 4K resolution and edited by a team of professionals, which gives it a professional look. There are many companies out there. Do your research and check them out before spending the money. It's an investment, but one that's worth it when professional jobs are on the line.

You want your child to succeed in their professional and artistic endeavors. Demo reels can open up unimaginable doors with an honest and memorable performance. Whether you are using TV clips, independent or student films, or original content, it's important to gather material that features your child at the center and showcases your child's talents. Your goal is to support your child's dream. Creating a great demo reel is one important tool in an arsenal of many that can jumpstart your child's career. You can see an example of teen actor Gabriel Rush's demo reel here: www.vimeo.com/210292804.

6. Supportive Family

All of the elements I have discussed are important to your child's acting career, but none so much as having family support. Professional acting is a full-time job, and it requires support and encouragement from everyone. Rejection is a large part of the entertainment industry; with every success your child experiences, multiple failures precede it. Acting takes a remarkable amount of courage and determination. It's an industry in which you need to believe wholeheartedly in your abilities as a performer. For your child to succeed, take a leap of faith as a family and encourage each other on this fantastic journey.

Sisters Hayley and Tori Feinstein have been in a wide variety of movies, commercials, television shows, and live theater. As of this writing, Hayley just ended her run in *Fiddler on the Roof* on

Broadway and Tori just finished playing the title role in *Matilda* on Broadway. I sat down with their parents, Jonathan and Cheryl, and asked them about how they got into the industry. The Feinsteins laughed and said they had no idea what they were doing or how things worked. Hayley had talent and enjoyed performing in local musical theater classes. They were at a charity auction at the local public school and bid on an appointment with an agent. They won the auction item and made an appointment for Hayley, who was in the second grade at the time.

Hayley was signed right away and subsequently booked a job doing voice-over work for a Disney animated television show, and soon after that, a role in the first national tour of *Shrek The Musical – Broadway*. Tori followed in her sister's footsteps, working in television and film, and eventually played the role of a lifetime, Matilda. Cheryl shared, "Honestly, when we started it, we thought acting was a nice extracurricular activity just like you would take a class or play a sport. We didn't realize at the time what a big commitment it was, that it wasn't just like a little extracurricular activity."

Websites

After your child has had some success and landed some roles, consider creating a website where all the materials discussed above can be found in one convenient spot. This is just another way for casting directors and directors to learn more about your young performer and see them in action. Add the website address to their resume. My clients, sisters Haley and Ashley Lanzoni, have outstanding websites. Take a look here: www.haleylanzoni.com and www.ashleylanzoni.com.

Now that you understand some of the emotional and practical aspects involved in helping your child get started, let's discuss how to get representation from an agent and a manager. Turn to chapter 8 and we'll begin.

Life Lessons = Success

- Preparing emotionally and practically is important for any new endeavor.

- Ask for help from those with experience and expertise when you don't know how to do something.

- You can never be perfect, but you can always grow and improve.

- Getting what you want requires an investment of time and energy.

- Success requires a progression of small steps taken over time.

Chapter 8

Getting Representation

Real acting is impossible to spot. Do you ever catch talents like Robert Duvall or Kathy Bates acting? No. I defy you to show me where.

— William Esper

Kim Lanzoni is the mother of two working child actresses, Haley and Ashley, who have been featured on stage and in film, television, voice-overs, commercials, and modeling. They are blessed with skills in acting, singing, and dance and have worked hard to hone their skills in all three areas. Kim and her daughters recently moved to New York from Boston.

I asked Kim about some of the sacrifices she's made for the girls' careers. She shared, "There are tremendous sacrifices, such as the time that's away from your family, the financial, and the things our girls gave up: their friends, being in school, giving up being in their own home. Those seem like simple things, but in the grand scheme of things, it's a big sacrifice. I am giving up things; I'm giving up my friends. I'm luckily in a wonderful relationship with my husband. He is living in Boston while I live in New York to take care of the kids. We've split our family up. He has been the most supportive husband. He comes to New York once every week or once every two weeks. Thanks to technology the kids can connect with him nearly every day whether it's by text or by FaceTime. That keeps our family feeling normal."

Because there are so many demands on the parents of child actors, Kim feels it's vital to build a team of support. She said, "As a parent, you don't know what you don't know. It took me a very long time to figure this all out. Talk to as many people as possible and start your kids as young as possible. Even if it's just coaching and you're not sure about going to New York, start them with just simple coaching, whether it's with the acting coach, your voice coach, your dance teacher. That is a great start because the prime age for kids I would say is between ages seven and twelve. Then it all starts to fall off from there. It's really hard to find auditions once you turn thirteen, fourteen, and certainly deeper into the teen years. My other advice is to approach everything as a team effort whether it is putting your team of agents together or your team of coaches. I approach everything with a team feeling. I want to surround myself with the people that I like, that I trust, that I feel are committed and believe in my kids."

Two of the most influential roles in your child's success team are the agent and the manager, who can share in the representation of your child. Some actors have only an agent, some a manager, and some both. As a talent manager, acting coach, and mentor to my students, the importance of good representation is always at the top of my list.

Getting the Attention of a Potential Representative

Agents and managers generally frequent theatrical productions, as they are always on the hunt for new talent. If your child is serious about acting professionally, make sure they are involved in school plays, community theater, and even regional theater. Reps are always looking for a child who has potential.

- **Industry showcases:** Industry showcases are perfect opportunities for young performers to gain industry attention. These are events in which agents, managers, and casting directors watch actors perform exclusively for them. Actors perform scenes, monologues, and songs, and even read commercial copy. If a rep is interested in your child, they will arrange a meeting and possibly sign on a new client. Even if your child doesn't sign with an agent or manager, they might keep their name on file to be seen again in the future.

- **Workshops and master classes:** Many acting workshops and master classes culminate with an informal performance for an agent or manager. These are generally for educational purposes. Your child practices in an audition-like setting. However, if an agent or manager sees promise in a performer, they might ask for their name to set up an interview.

- **Old-fashioned mailings:** Years ago agents and managers primarily gained clients through headshots and resumes mailed to them by hopeful performers. (See chapter 7 for information about resumes and headshots.) Get a list of agents and managers who work with young performers through *Backstage's* Callsheet, at www.backstage.com/resources, and send a hard copy to them with a short cover letter. If you live outside of the big industry cities, call your local SAG-AFTRA office to get the names of reputable agents.

- **Referrals:** Perhaps you have a friend whose child is signed with an agency or management company. Ask for a referral. This can get your foot in the door faster than mailings because the agent can ask questions and gain a sense of who you are from a person they already know and trust.

- **Your coaches:** Your acting or voice teacher can refer you to a rep. I never pass up an opportunity to send one of my promising young students to one of my colleagues if I believe they are ready to work. Since the young actor has been vetted by me, the rep is more apt to respond. I have introduced many of my students to both agents and managers who have worked together to create successful careers.

How to Choose a Representative

Choosing a representative – agent or manager – is like choosing a pediatrician. Do your research, ask questions, and trust your gut.

First you must know what's right for your child. Their representative should be caring, supportive, and believe in your child's potential for success. It can be hard to know if you should start looking for an agent or a manager first. My advice is to interview both agents and managers and see who is most interested in your child. Remember that you are interviewing for team members who can support your child's career. Agents and managers are looking for talent and marketability.

Interviews generally have two portions. Your child will be asked to meet privately with the potential representative, who will assess their skills, look, and marketability. You'll then meet with them to talk about the business aspects of representation. Your child can participate in the business interview if they are old enough.

The Talent Interview

There is always an intangible aspect to stardom. Charisma is hard to define, but we all know it when we see it. As Bonnie Shumofsky, a top child agent with Abrams Artists in New York, said, "Identifying young talent is a process. As in many professions, there is a combination of the so-called art and science. The science aspect is what is tangible. The art, however, is having an eye for what I call the 'wow factor.' It may be from a performance I see or even just a conversation during a meeting. It is very hard to put this piece of the process into words, and as with most art, it's more a measure of sensing and being in tune with the emotional impact generated by a young artist. That's what I look for."

The representative will evaluate your child's personality at all times, looking for the sparkle that only a diamond has. They will look at three primary areas:

1. **Confidence:** There is no substitute for confidence. It affects everything about a person's demeanor – face, voice, body language – and every interaction. David Gilbert, talent agent with Zuri Model and Talent Agency in New York, said, "I am always looking for someone who is going to 'win the room' – when they walk into my office, they've got to have confidence. Also, they've got to be directable, able to make adjustments on the spot." When a young performer believes in themselves, they not only make a great impression but are better able to take direction during an audition or taping and to respond appropriately to unexpected situations or requests. Being self-assured puts others at ease and transmits confidence to an audience. It is something that can be developed over time with experience, yet even a young person can dig deep and project more confidence than they might feel in the moment.

2. **Marketability:** Barry Kolker, of The Carson Kolker Organization, knows there has to be a market for each young performer in his stable. "When signing children and teen actors, I look for a 'type' that I need, so that I don't have 'conflicts' and submit too many clients." This is often a matter of timing, so keep in mind that while your child's look might not be in demand today, things could change tomorrow. It could also mean that one person already represents someone with this particular look, and there will be others looking to fill the same spot in their own rosters. Persevere. Markets are fluid, and young performers evolve as they grow up, so over time they find themselves positioned differently depending on many factors.

3. Parental support: Kolker goes on to say, "I look for talented kids/teens with a lot of personality who have a passion for performing and whose parent or guardian can make the commitment. I'm looking for a family who I feel will be easy to work with and that I feel/hope that we can be successful together!" David Gilbert agrees, saying, "I want parents who support their child and are encouraging, who understand that their job is to be a good parent and mine is to be a good agent." You are an essential ingredient for success, and agents know it. Make sure they understand that you are committed and willing to do what it takes so that you all succeed in the end.

Ellen Gilbert, a top agent at Paradigm Talent Agency in New York, added, "I'm looking to find that special something, that 'it factor' that really just pops as soon as you meet a kid and you know immediately, she has talent and potential." I agree with Gilbert. It's hard to define that "it factor," but experienced agents, managers, and casting directors know it when they see it. It's not something you can teach your child, but helping them feel confident and comfortable allows their natural talent to shine.

Interview Preparation

Your child might be nervous, thinking, "If I am just plain old me, will I make enough of an impression?" They should be prepared and able to be themselves. Have them look their best in attractive but comfortable clothing. Remind them to relax and have a good time.

Each representative has their own process for interviewing. Your child should be prepared with a monologue (and songs if they sing), and be able to *cold-read*, which means reading something they have not seen before. The songs should be ones they love to sing that show some contrast, such as a pop or up-tempo song and a slower ballad.

It's a good idea to practice interviewing with your child so they become comfortable providing full answers to questions using complete sentences and relaxing into a natural conversation. Remind them not to give one-word answers. Above all, your child should be prepared enough to feel calm and comfortable.

I once judged a beauty pageant. For the interview section I was one of two judges in a small room. A young girl came in and said grandly, "Hello Ladies and Gentlemen." I asked for her name and she repeated, "Hello Ladies and Gentlemen," as if she were a little robot. Prepare your child to do the interview without you present so they're not surprised by anything. Most children do best without their parent present because they don't have to worry about disappointing them.

The Parent Interview

Get familiar with the company you are interviewing with beforehand. Research it on the web and ask colleagues what they know about it. You will feel more self-assured if you prepare questions ahead of time.

You might feel flattered and excited to be interviewing with the representative, but remember, *you* (and your child) are hiring *them*. Ask questions, get informed, and listen carefully. This is an important decision and you want to make sure this person is a good fit. The personality of your representative does matter! They need to work for your child *and* you, so their personality should meld with both of yours. At the end of the day, everyone involved has to feel comfortable.

Here are some questions you might want to ask a potential representative:

- **What do you see as my child's type?**
  This is a crucial question and one that needs to be discussed before signing a contract. Your daughter might think she can play the girl next door, yet your potential representative sees

her as the quirky best friend. Now is the time to get on the same page. Discuss whether your child will be sent to theater as well as television and film auditions. Do you both agree that comedy is your child's thing? And if it is, will they still be considered for one-hour dramas and film as well? If they're interested in pursuing commercials and voice-overs, find out if someone different in the agency handles that, and if so, who.

- **How many clients do you have and how many are the same type as my child?**
  Agencies and management companies come in all sizes. Some have a handful of clients; some have hundreds. Find out how many other represented clients are your child's type and how that might affect getting submitted for projects.

- **How do you feel about me or my child submitting them for projects ourselves?**
  There are many ways to find out about projects without going through a representative. There are open calls listed in online resources and trade publications. While a representative will work hard to secure auditions, you might find something they do not know about. Ask how they like to handle this. What about student films? Find out if they're open to your child pursuing these leads.

- **Do you recommend photographers and acting, voice, and dance teachers?** There are a plethora of photographers and teachers out there. Ask what this potential representative thinks of your child's current headshot and who takes their clients' fabulous pictures. Find out where some of their other clients study acting, voice, and dance. It's always great to get a personal recommendation when you can.

- **If I sign with you as a manager, do I need to be signed with one agent or will I freelance with many?**
  Years ago managers submitted actors directly for projects without an agent and used an attorney to negotiate the contract.

This is still a gray area. Some continue to work this way, and in the kids' world it is common to work with a manager and freelance with a few agents. Whichever agent calls the manager for the client first gets to submit the actor for an audition. Today many managers sign their clients to one agent and collaborate with that agent as a team. Find out how your prospective representative works and ensure it will meet your child's needs.

- **What is the difference between a freelance agreement and signing with you?**
  It is typical to sign a one-year exclusive contract with an agent and a three-year contract with a manager. It is also possible to work *on a handshake,* a *verbal exclusive,* or *freelance* with several agents. Being under contract can give you a sense of security, knowing your representative is committed to your child. Regardless, be sure to ask the person you are interviewing how their company operates and determine whether it will work for you.

- **Do you have other clients working? What projects are they involved in?**
  Be sure that the representative is current in the child-actor industry and has the much-needed connections for your child's success. Ensure that they have the "bandwidth" to manage your child's career.

- **What did you see in my child that you liked?**

- **How can I help in this process?**

- **How do you prefer to be contacted?** Reps are busy working to get their clients auditions. Find out if they prefer to be contacted by phone or email, and how often.

After the interview, be sure to ask your child how they felt about the representative. It is important that both your child and you feel good about them. It is a relationship, and hopefully one that will last a long time.

Should You Manage Your Child's Career?

Working as a manager is a very demanding role. It requires an in-depth understanding of the industry, keen organizational skills, marketing savvy, strong communication skills, and the ability to develop relationships with principal industry players. Most parents don't have the industry knowledge or contacts to be effective managers unless they have already worked in the industry.

Kim Pedell of ZOOM Talent Management is a professional talent manager. When I spoke to her about parents managing their children's careers, she said, "Managers can be very helpful when giving advice before an audition. Sometimes they have more information because they have already been working on the project or because they know the casting director well. A parent cannot be as objective when giving feedback. It's also difficult for a parent not to take it personally when their child does not book a job. It's so important for young actors to do their very best in the room and then forget about it. Often parents become much more invested because of time and sometimes money spent in preparation, and it can put pressure on a young actor. "

If you're thinking of managing your child's career, consider these questions:

- Do you have industry connections and experience?
- Are you able to negotiate contracts knowledgeably?
- Can you separate your emotions from your child's and help them cope effectively with rejection?
- Will you be able to care for your other family members and stay involved with them while you are devoting your time to career management?

In my experience the most important role of a parent is to parent. You will be monitoring their emotions, health, life balance, and enjoyment of the industry because you know your child better than anyone else. You are the best person to provide support, ensure that your child still has normal childhood experiences, and advocate for them with other team members. Your love is the anchor that will help them cope with the demands of working in an adult world. So unless you are an industry insider, focus your efforts on being your child's best parent and advocate. Work alongside a representative you trust and the other members of your child's team. Your contribution is vital and valuable to your child's success. Acting careers come and go, but your role as a parent lasts forever!

More Thoughts about Your Role

Your behavior and attitude during interviews really matters. Representatives do not want to work with demanding, unpleasant, or uncommunicative parents. Elise Koseff is a manager with MKS&D Talent Management, with offices in New York and Los Angeles, and is responsible for the careers of many award-winning actors. She has been representing actors and developing talent for over thirty years. I asked Elise for some tips for parents who want to have great relationships with their representatives. Elise said:

> Parents need to be really vigilant about answering emails, answering questions, confirming auditions, making sure they go on absolutely everything that they possibly can. It's a numbers game. The thing is, this industry works so fast that if you weren't available one day you may have missed that big Steven Spielberg film that you might have booked or an opportunity to be featured in that big TV series. Parents also often have to know how to deal with technology. You have to be able to self-tape your child from home. You have to do it well. You need to make sure your child is prepared for all auditions. Sometimes I hear that a child walked in the room and they never looked at the material. Scripts have to be read and understood. It is a lot of work. This is not an easy business.

Elise reminds parents that listening to the advice of their representatives is critical. There are times when a representative urges a child not to take a job based on inside knowledge they have about the people involved or other factors they may not be able to share. Representatives know how to communicate effectively with a variety of casting directors. Parents can unwittingly cause a problem in their child's career when they approach directors personally or cause issues.

As you can see, finding the right agent and/or manager for your child is a matter of preparation, research, and intuition. These valuable team members will have a significant influence on your child's success, so search until you find just the right people for your child's team.

If you have a relationship with a representative that is not working, it's okay to take some action. One of my clients recently came to me for advice because her agent was not sending her to many auditions and had become uncommunicative. She and her family were getting frustrated with the lack of effort and communication they were receiving. I suggested finding a new agent. The family followed my suggestion and I am happy to report that the young lady just booked a role in a Nickelodeon television series. Sometimes a fresh perspective is important.

Life Lessons = Success

- Interviewing is a skill that you can master with practice and preparation.
- Learning how to have a conversation when meeting people for the first time will help you in every area of life. Be friendly and approachable.
- Trust your gut and ask yourself how you feel about working with a particular person.
- Be yourself in every situation. Honesty is always the best policy.
- Don't be afraid to speak up when a relationship isn't working.

Chapter 9

Practical Audition Tips

You're not going there to get a job. You're going there to present what you do.

— Bryan Cranston

Noah Fleiss has been acting for almost thirty years. He started at age seven in a Broadway play and was cast in a film at age eight. His parents, Karen and Mitchell Fleiss, have done a great job raising Noah and his sister Brittany. (More about the Fleisses in chapter 11.) Karen is a child psychologist who was able to use her professional training to help prepare Noah for the challenges of auditions. She shared, "As parents, we tried to model the acceptance of the rejection. If a particular role was something he wanted, we would want it as well; but we would also let him know that if he gave it his best shot and he wasn't selected, that's okay. You have to go into auditions with an understanding that you can do all the right things, and yet not get the job. As parents, it's important to keep a positive and appropriate perspective, and make sure to keep it in its place." Mitchell added that they were very careful as parents to watch Noah and make sure that he knew acting was a part of his life, but not his entire life. That's a healthy perspective for both children and parents to take to auditions.

What Do Casting Directors Want?

According to the Casting Society of America (CSA), casting directors are hired by studios, networks or production companies and are employed to present actors for consideration. Casting Directors also negotiate, on behalf of those companies, the deals to hire the actors selected.

For aspiring and working actors, casting directors are the golden tickets to getting seen, networking with industry leaders, and booking jobs. The question I'm asked most often is what do casting directors look for in young performers. Casting directors see thousands of children and know what makes an artist a standout. I have worked with casting directors throughout my entire career and can lend some insight on their process.

1. **Naturalness:** Acting may be pretend and make-believe, but that does not mean your child should seem fake. In show business it's important not to be "show-bizzy." Casting directors aren't interested in "jazz hands" and costumes, but kids being themselves. Jen Rudin, CSA, an award-winning casting director and author, emphasized the importance of authenticity in auditions: "Be yourself. I always respond to the kids who are real and not manufactured in their acting or personality. I can spot a fake young actor from a mile away, so just relax and be you!" It is important that the casting director sees your young performer with an authentic personality and an emotional connection to their audition materials.

2. **Personality:** Acting natural does not mean toning down your personality. In fact, it's what casting directors are most eager to see! Is your child funny, thoughtful, interesting, quirky? These are all-important pieces of your child's temperament that help a casting director place them in their head as the character for which they are casting. Joy Dewing, CSA, said, "As a mother, it is of paramount importance to me that the

child wants to be there, and that their parents are supporting them, not pushing them." Seeing a child open up and connect with a casting director by demonstrating their passion for the craft is sometimes the most valuable aspect of an audition. It makes a child memorable – and that's no small thing when competing with thousands of hopefuls for a part.

3. **Professionalism**: It requires a certain level of maturity for a child to be a professional actor. Unlike other young children, they have a career to cultivate and maintain. Acting is fun, but it is also a job. Casting directors want to see that a child they hire will be easy to work with and will bring positive things to a set. Casting director Merri Sugarman, CSA, works for one of the largest casting companies in New York, Tara Rubin Casting. Sugarman and her team are responsible for casting children in Broadway shows like *A Bronx Tale, Falsettos, Miss Saigon, School of Rock,* and *Les Miserables.* She also casts children for national touring companies, regional theaters, television pilots, and movies. I asked Sugarman what she looks for in a child actor. She replied, "We're looking for kids who seem mature in temperament. Acting is a challenging business and we feel protective of the kids we're hiring. I'm also assessing if they can go above and beyond just playing the part by getting a feel for their home lives and the kind of support that they get from their parents and guardians." Casting directors recognize and value the children with whom they do business. Competition is so fierce for young performers; there's no room for divas or immaturity in the industry.

4. **Well-roundedness**: Professional acting at any age is a full-time job, but there is still time for kids to grow in other areas of their lives. Stephanie Klapper, CSA, said, "The kids we love to cast are those who are enormously talented but are still real kids! They genuinely love performing but have other

interests, too. They do it because they love it, not because they (or their parents) want them to be famous." Your child's interests outside of acting can be as essential in an audition as their song or monologue. If your child has skills in other areas, it is to their advantage to continue with them. More important, they allow casting directors to see all the wonderful parts that make up your child.

5. **Training**: A young performer may have a winning look and a great personality, but those will fall short in an audition without proper training. Whether it is through group classes or private coaching, it is essential that young actors build a foundation in the theater arts. Jason Styres, CSA, talks of understanding audition material when casting children: "My main focus is seeing the natural learning process on which each kid thrives. That is the only way I can figure out how to approach whatever material they have brought in."

Casting directors are looking for a well-rounded, authentic child who can bring their acting chops to the table and give a compelling performance. One of the most helpful things your child can do to prepare for an audition is learn the material. That means being familiar enough with the material that they can present it smoothly, only glancing down at the script for reference. Children must be able to listen and follow instructions, so the more familiar they are with the material, the easier it is to incorporate additional instructions.

By the way, you are being assessed, too. A parent's behavior can influence casting decisions. If two children are being considered for a role and one parent is easier to work with, their child could win the part over the one who has a demanding or intrusive parent. Sugarman shared, "You want there to be harmony on stage as well as offstage. Parents of child actors play a big role in that. Even if one child is more talented than another, many times they will be passed over if their parent seems like someone who will create problems."

Preparing for the Audition

Your child (or you if they are not old enough) should read the entire script, or at least everything that has been provided. Many times a *breakdown*, a description of the project that includes a storyline synopsis in addition to descriptions of all the characters/roles in the script, is provided. Be sure to review the entire scene and the stage directions to get as much information as possible. This helps them understand the character and the situation. Agent Ellen Gilbert concurs, suggesting that older children read the entire script, not just the *sides*, which are the specific lines an actor should learn for an audition.

Memorization

There are a few schools of thought on memorizing lines for auditions. My general rule of thumb is if you can memorize and memorize well, then do it. That means knowing the lines so well that you don't have to think about them. If, however, the actor doesn't have the lines down solidly, they should be very familiar with them, only glancing at the script when necessary. This requires practice in how to work with a script. It should be used as an aid only.

If the audition is taped or your child is invited to a callback, they MUST memorize the lines. This ensures they are connecting with the *reader* (the person who reads the other part or parts during the audition), not the script. It demonstrates to the casting director that your child is truly a professional and on top of their game in a very competitive industry, and helps them give the best performance possible.

Here's where it gets tricky: If the actor gets fifteen pages of copy the night before and kind of has it memorized and tries to audition from memory, they will be trying to remember the next line rather than being fully present to the reader and listening for direction.

No one is penalized for not fully memorizing the script. Casting directors would much rather see a child connecting to the character than knowing the words perfectly.

However, reading and acting are completely different. A person can be a great reader but a so-so actor, and vice versa. If reading is getting in the way of acting, your child should memorize the lines to have a successful audition. One of the most challenging things for young performers – especially first and second graders – is reading naturally when auditioning. Since these young ones are still relatively new readers, they often get stuck on words, and the reading becomes unnatural. If they memorize the lines, this takes the task of reading away, and they can concentrate on being authentic.

Here are some tips to help you keep your sanity while helping your child memorize lines, or at least be very familiar with them:

- **Highlight the character's lines.** This allows your child to quickly locate the appropriate line if they need to glance down at the paper during the audition.
- **Repetition.** Have your child read the lines with someone out loud over and over again. Remind them to memorize the lines only, not the cadence and inflection. They need to discover something new each time they read the lines – saying them as if they are spoken for the first time, each time.
- **Break down lines into smaller pieces.** Don't have your child tackle the entire script all at once. Break the script down into small sections and repeat, repeat, repeat until the lines are ingrained.
- **Work on lines before going to sleep**. Studies have shown that studying lines right before going to sleep can have a significant impact on recall. Be sure to have your child review them again in the morning to help lock them into memory.

Remember that memorizing is only one tool for your child to use in an audition. Remind your child that connecting with the reader is more important than the words they say, and if they don't get the line exactly as written, it is totally normal. Making the scene their own with specific choices, as well as being able to listen and take direction, are what helps them get the attention they need and ultimately land the job.

While your child is working on preparing their lines, guide them to think about the characters and their motivations. Encourage them to read the entire script, including stage directions, to get a feel for what's happening in the scene. Make it a game and ask your child to describe the characters in the scene using verbs such as *manipulating, begging, playing,* and *taunting,* and to visualize what the characters are doing physically.

When you help your child go beyond just the words and examine the script in this way, they will be able to decide how they want to approach the material. There are no wrong answers. Encourage them to portray the character as honestly as they can.

Wardrobe

I recommend that kids dress in the *flavor* of the character. If your young performer is playing an edgy or rebellious teen, perhaps jeans and a black top. If they are playing a quirky, artistic type, choose a colorful, fun outfit. I never recommend going in a costume; it looks as if they are trying too hard. Clothing should not take the focus, as the attention needs to be on your child, not their attire. However, your child's appearance should help them connect with the character.

For taped or filmed auditions, avoid stripes, busy patterns, and logos, as these are very distracting. For period pieces, I recommend a dark skirt and white blouse for a girl and khakis and a polo shirt for a boy. Find colors that work well for your child, bring out their eyes, and make them feel good.

The right shoes are critical. Young performers often slush about, kick their feet, and weave from side to side. Help your child learn to stand firmly rooted, signaling that they are ready and prepared to do their best. Never have your child wear flip-flops, thick wooly boots, platform shoes, or extremely high heels. Shoes should be age appropriate and not distract in any way. The best shoes are flat, comfortable, and fit well so that your child can move easily and feel well-grounded.

I spoke with Kaitlin Hopkins, head of the musical theater program at Texas State University, on the subject, and here is what she had to say: "I often see young women who wear very high heels and deprive themselves of two important opportunities. First, to be grounded and not teeter on top of stilettos that prevent them from anchoring their breath. They also inhibit movement, which can then come across as stiff and stilted. And second, it takes away the opportunity for us to imagine them as different characters. It is harder for us to imagine them as multiple characters if the actor overdresses and doesn't seem comfortable and able to move freely."

Three Tips to Help Young Actors Make Better First Impressions

It has often been said that a casting director sizes you up the minute you walk through the door. It turns out that research from Princeton University showed this to be wrong. It only takes about a tenth of a second! To me, there are two fascinating things about this. First, they make these judgments not just about appearance, but about a whole host of traits. Second, these quick impressions last; additional evaluation time usually only increases their confidence in their judgments.

Talk about pressure! This can make not only young actors nervous but also their parents. And that often leads to trying to make everything perfect with rehearsed answers to expected questions. Unfortunately all that does is take the spontaneity and interest out of your child. Instead, follow these three tips to help your young actor make their first impression a good one:

1. **Practice at home.** Help your young actor get comfortable talking about subjects that are likely to come up in a casting call such as their hobbies, siblings, pets, school, and friends. Focus less on specific answers and more on their feeling comfortable with the topics. Aside from guiding your child away from blatantly inappropriate or one-word responses, let their unaffected honesty, clarity, and personality show. That is what casting directors want to see come through.

2. **For younger actors, make a game out of it.** Get a group of friends and family to pretend they are meeting for the first time. Have each person speak with another for a few minutes and then write a one- or two-word positive "first impression" on a card taped to their partner's back. Then have them pick a new partner and repeat until all the participants have written something on everyone's card. Have each person reveal what others said about them and discuss what we communicate when we first meet another person. This is a fun way to cover many basics of good communication such as eye contact, smiling, listening, posture, courtesy, and many others.

3. **Take your teen to the mall.** Once your young actor feels comfortable talking about themselves while role playing with family and friends, it's time to practice with strangers. If your child participates in baseball, for example, head to a sporting goods store and have them talk to a clerk about the equipment they use, what they like and don't like about it, and what the salesperson recommends. Your goal is to help your child practice and feel comfortable creating rapport with adults they do not know.

Despite the fact that these are important life skills, for most children and many adults they do not come naturally. Follow these tips to give your child the communication skills and confidence to make the casting interview a positive experience. Combined with talent and solid acting training, this practice will put your young actor in the best possible position to land many wonderful new roles.

Audition No-Nos for the Young Performer

All performers want the one audition secret that will guarantee them a fabulous role. But sometimes it's not what you do, but what you don't do that makes the difference. This is especially true for young performers and their parents who deal with the natural, emotional ups and downs of childhood. Here are a few tips to make a big difference at your child's auditions:

- **Don't bring the entire family.** Auditioning is exciting for the whole family, but the reality is that they can be a minefield of family friction with long periods of waiting that go through lunch and finish in rush-hour traffic. Young actors demonstrate maturity and perform at their best without an entourage.

- **Don't shake hands unless a hand is extended.** Staying healthy is a priority when you work with hundreds of child actors daily who don't reliably wash their hands. In general, casting directors prefer and appreciate a warm greeting without the handshake.

- **Don't speak for your child.** Don't be the reason a casting director overlooks the articulate, independent qualities of your child because you interrupted, corrected, or asked questions that could have waited until later. Give them a chance to develop rapport with your child and your child will be much more likely to have audition success.

- **Discourage swinging legs.** A very young performer's feet often swing to and fro because they don't reach the floor when sitting. This makes a child look fidgety. Have your child practice sitting farther forward in the seat. This should allow them to rest their feet comfortably on the floor while sitting with a good, natural posture.

- **Don't coach a phony.** Poor coaching advice from well-meaning adults can result in an insincere audition. It is obvious when a child actor is coached on exactly what to say regardless of what is said to them. And don't coach them to look directly into the camera rather than at the reader or scene partner. If they avoid anything that is unnatural, the audition is likely to feel sincere.

A parent's guidance, support, and encouragement play vital roles in a young actor's career. Remember to guide gently, support quietly, and encourage consistently. This gives your child the best opportunity to develop the audition skills that land the next great role.

Open Casting Calls

Almost every successful actor in the business began by attending open casting calls, when casting directors open their doors to the acting public. No agent or manager is required. These are opportunities for undiscovered talent to gain experience and exposure. I highly recommend that children who are starting out go to open casting calls for a couple of reasons: they might be discovered; and they might discover they do not like acting. You can find out about open casting calls and other resources at some of these reputable sites:

- **Backstage.com:** There is no place I recommend more than *Backstage*. This casting platform leads the pack for actors finding work. They post thousands of auditions for actors, singers, and dancers, not to mention openings for film crews. You can search by location and use the many filters to find auditions suitable for your child. *Backstage* allows users to narrow audition criteria by age, compensation, ethnicity, role type, and many other parameters. It saves time by updating you with auditions customized to your child's needs. In addition to acting opportunities, *Backstage* has expert advice columns and links for finding acting coaches, voice teachers, production companies, headshot photographers, and many other resources. I write a regular column for *Backstage* for young actors and their families.

- **ActorsAccess.com:** Actors Access is designed specifically for actors. Actors upload their headshots and resumes and can submit their portfolios electronically through the website. There's a "Pay as you go" option through Showfax, a companion website, where you can pay $2.00 for each submission or a flat fee of $68 per year for unlimited submissions. The real gem of Actors Access is the availability of audition sides. If a casting director uploads the sides to their site posting, you can download the audition materials instead of waiting to hear from the casting director or their representative.

- **Playbill.com:** Playbill has long been the must-read for theatergoers everywhere. Created in 1884 for a New York theater, it has since evolved into a hub of theater history, current events, and, thanks to its website, casting opportunities. Playbill does not offer a subscription service for electronic submissions; instead, it lists in detail the audition information, materials, and location. Playbill is an excellent resource for performers interested in theater, and, most important, it's free! In today's age, when actors are required to pay for most everything, Playbill is a valuable tool for tomorrow's theater stars.

- **Castingnetworks.com:** Casting Networks offers actors a state of the art site for posting their headshots, resumes, and demo reels. Casting directors flock to it because its scheduling software makes it easy for casting directors to see actors. Actors are given a custom URL and can upload up to fifty pictures and unlimited media clips of up to four minutes.

What's most valuable to actors is the Casting Networks Talent Scout feature. It's free for users who have a personal account. Actors specify the type of representation they're looking for, and they are then searchable by prospective agents and managers.

- **Nowcasting.com:** Now Casting is an online video audition site that also provides other resources to members. Actors post a free profile consisting of a video audition and actor profile, and can send it securely and privately to casting directors. Casting directors can also post casting calls. Once you have a profile, you can access free sides if you are a union member.

- **Mandy.com:** Mandy provides a comprehensive guide to independent-film and TV-production resources. It includes a detailed directory of 100,000+ production companies, filmmakers, production crews, and equipment as well as a casting directory of audition opportunities in the US and international markets.

- **CastingFrontier.com:** Casting Frontier uses technology to move the audition process online. It is also the first company to develop a comprehensive set of mobile casting tools specifically designed for the iPad, iPhone, and Android. These revolutionary apps include iSession Mobile, Director on the Go, Agent on the Go, and Actor on the Go. Actors can choose a free account or upgrade to a paid account that allows for posting a more robust profile. Once you have a profile, you will be notified of audition opportunities that match your profile.

Since you may not have the support of an agent or manager, be your child's advocate and use your good judgment to carefully screen these casting opportunities for legitimacy and appropriateness.

Life Lessons = Success

- Accept constructive feedback and use it to improve.

- Preparation is an important component of success.

- Learn to talk to adults in a friendly but respectful way.

- Gain responsibility by researching opportunities on your own.

- Your appearance is important and contributes to people's overall impression of who you are. Celebrate your differences!

Chapter 10

Coping with Rejection

If you live in the past that's depression,
and if you live in the future that's anxiety.
So you have no choice but to live in the present.

— Sarah Silverman

David Quinn started his acting career at age four when he landed a role on *Sesame Street*. He went on to work steadily in television and commercials for thirty years. He credits his manager and agent for telling him he'd always be a character actor – the chubby kid or the friend with the big glasses and funny hair. He knew his type from early on – what he calls "The Second Banana."

David auditioned frequently, sometimes even several times each week. He said, "I also knew that NO was something I was going to hear more than anything. I was blessed with a mother who said, 'There are many two-letter words. There's over a hundred two-letter words and NO is only one of them.' She said, 'You can flip it because the opposite of NO is to be ON. Another two-letter word is UP. If you want to fixate on two-letter words, you have other ones you can fixate on.' I never looked back after hearing that."

Today David is an educator and entrepreneur in Seattle. He co-founded Allrecipes.com, the most popular food website in the world. He is living his dream of working with high school students and investing in new business ventures. Because he works with talented teens, he has a unique perspective on rejection. He believes rejection is good for kids in many ways, and shared, "Rejection is a way to understand that you don't measure yourself based on what other people think. You measure yourself based on how you view yourself. I understood that NO was just one person's ideal, one person's opinion, that there were millions of people out there, that if I took in every NO and owned every NO, I'd just sit in the chair all day waiting for an experience to happen to me. A NO is, I mean it sounds kind of absurd, but a NO is simply an opportunity to find a YES." David found that he was auditioning several times a week for some casting directors and that a No on Monday could be a Yes on Thursday.

Dealing with the pressures of auditioning and being rejected is one of the most challenging parts of the entertainment business. Your role is to help your child navigate the experiences of being selected and rejected and to help them cope with the emotions that arise from both of these events. In this chapter you'll learn how to help your child cope with the ups and downs of auditioning.

Embracing Rejection

In a culture that is doing away with the winners and losers – in which everybody gets a ribbon or a trophy – our children are entering adulthood not understanding that "just showing up" isn't always enough. While consistently showing up can demonstrate perseverance and dedication, it takes more than that to win a role.

Beyond that, many kids have been subtly taught that making a fuss can get them what they want – or that an adult will step in to intervene and force circumstances in their favor; that a no is somehow negotiable if you have the right leverage. But in the adult world there are times when you don't win – you don't get the job, the offer on the house isn't accepted, the client says no, or your date stands you up. How can kids learn to accept rejection without going into meltdown? After all, nobody likes to be told no, but that doesn't mean it's not going to happen. Graciously accepting rejection, and being able to learn from it and move on, is a life skill. As with most skills, it takes practice, and where better to get that practice than in show business?!

There are many things that make this a tough industry, but the steep competition is one of the biggest. No one likes being passed over, left out, or told they are not "right." Still, competition is a fact of life, and the better we are at handling rejection, the easier it is to stay competitive as we grow up. There are several important lessons to be learned from every failure, every rejection.

Dr. Jay Berk is a child psychologist in private practice and was a consultant to the Young Performers Committee of the Screen Actors Guild for many years. I asked him about how rejection impacts children. He stated that learning to cope with rejection is an important developmental milestone for all children. Sometime during childhood or adolescence, every child is left out, not selected for a team, or has a falling out with a friend. Learning to cope with rejection helps children prepare for adulthood.

According to Berk, children in the entertainment industry can encounter rejection at a younger age and with greater frequency than other children. Parents need to prepare their young actors for rejection so that they see it as part of acting and nothing personal. These tips from Berk are especially useful:

- Help your child understand that there are many talented performers and that their acceptance or rejection might not be related to how well they performed during auditions. For example, casting directors might be looking for someone who is taller or shorter or has a different eye color. All these factors are outside of your child's control and have nothing to do with how well they performed.

- Teach your child to look around during auditions and consider how many other kids could be chosen for the part based on their looks. If the part calls for a blond-haired boy between the ages of six and ten, show your son that he is one of many candidates for the part.

- Help your child understand friendly competition. They will encounter many of the same kids in auditions, so teach them to be friendly and upbeat. If they can feel glad when a friend gets a role that they didn't, they will gain valuable coping skills and resiliency that will help them throughout life.

Praising your child for their efforts in preparing for auditions and their willingness to take risks is an important and constructive approach, advised Dr. Lisa Sussman:

> Listen to your child's words and encourage him or her to express feelings of disappointment without trying to take them away. Allowing your child to feel and learn to manage disappointing emotions is a critically important aspect of empowering your child with skills that will allow tolerance of future disappointments and challenges. Refrain from the urge to try to immediately "solve" your child's problems or take away the pain. Sharing a personal story of your own experience with rejection and how you coped with the disappointment can be very meaningful and can offer comfort and a healthy perspective to your child. Furthermore, after some time has passed it can be helpful to encourage your child to identify some specific areas to work on to continue to improve skills for future auditions. This proactive and positive approach, like that of learning to tolerate distress, is another step in empowering your child to continue to persist, be resilient and work hard. Remember that disappointment is a normal emotion, and developing appropriate and mature behaviors

in response to disappointment is a critical skill in the performance world, and in overall healthy development.

The Ugly Duckling Wasn't a Duck

Auditions are big unknowns. The actor walks into an audition with basic information and is asked to perform without knowing much about the context. This is scary and exciting – and a fact of life for actors.

Teach your child this one rule of auditioning: Be yourself – your unique, perfect self! Your job is to go for it! Do your best, don't worry about what you don't know, and go home happy. That said, professional acting is a creative business that has little to do with concrete rules and everything to do with the preferences of the people in charge. In addition to looking for acting skill, casting directors have a number of physical criteria for each part they are casting, such as age, height, weight, sex, ethnicity, and type. Sometimes young actors even need to resemble on-set family members who were already cast! It is not personal. There is nothing an actor can do about such factors.

You can't become a duck if you are a swan. No matter how talented and amazing a performer might be, casting choices are often based on completely arbitrary traits. Let your child know that the important things are to do their personal best on that day, and enjoy the process.

Kiss a Lot of Frogs to Find the Magic One

For every audition, the odds of landing a role are pretty slim. There are often hundreds of actors answering the call for an audition, yet only one will be cast. Every actor faces the same overwhelming odds and the likelihood of rejection. That means your child might have to go on hundreds of auditions – and get hundreds of rejections – for each part they get. But every no gets them that much closer to a yes.

There is a saying, "Never let the odds keep you from doing what you know you were meant to do." Actors are rejected many times before finding the right role at the right time with the right people. Success comes to those who keep their energy up and continue with confidence.

Navigating the entertainment industry requires a strong sense of self-confidence and a bit of thick skin. And for both child and parent it might seem easier to give in to the doubts and settle for a hobby that has more stability. But your child isn't just dabbling at this. It's not a hobby, it's a passion! As an artist they have made the bold decision to live for their passion. This is a positive decision that you can reinforce when they feel rejected.

Tomorrow Is a Brand New Day

Any kid in musical theater is familiar with *Annie*; she knows that the sun comes up tomorrow on a brand new day. Resilience is a life lesson that actors learn to accept and embrace because it is so critical to their way of life. Every time they try something, they risk failure. No matter what it is, the next step is the same: Try again!

Your job is to praise your child's efforts, hard work, and the courage they show every time they perform. Rehashing what went wrong, placing blame, getting lost in worry, or becoming frustrated or angry don't help. Keep those thoughts to yourself or share them with the manager or coach if you need to vent.

If your child gets caught up in second-guessing themselves, acknowledge their concerns and let them know you can relate. Share some things that you learned from your past "failures." Teach them that reviewing the past can be helpful as long as it is framed in a positive way. Make it a game to hunt for one or two nuggets of wisdom that will give them greater confidence in the future.

Be aware that you might take a rejection harder than your child does! Not every rejection needs to be a teaching moment. Resist the urge to deliver your "resilience builds character" lecture on the way home. If your child shrugs it off, you can, too. But if your child needs to talk about it, be a willing listener. Sometimes just venting is all they need to process what happened, move through disappointment, and move on. If they're wallowing in sadness, gently help them move forward by helping them identify a few positive things they learned that they can take into the next audition.

Another great idea is to create a fun, post-audition ritual to transition from the intensity of their performance back to other parts of life – pizza, a movie, a trip to the bookstore, or ice cream sundaes. Celebrate the day's achievements!

Let It Go!

Kids and adults alike can have a hard time letting go of a past disappointment. As someone with more life experience than your child, you know that the hurt, disappointment, and anger from a rejection are temporary feelings. While they're acute in the moment, the sooner you can let them go, the sooner you can move on. But to a child, well-meaning advice like "Just let it go!" and "This too shall pass" doesn't feel helpful. While a mature child might intellectually understand that not getting a part they really wanted isn't the end of the world – or their career, emotionally they're still mired in the moment.

Think back to when your child was a toddler and fell and scraped their knee. To you it was a minor injury that would soon be forgotten; but to your child, in that moment, it was terrifying, life-threatening, and it hurt! Telling a screaming two-year-old to "get over it" wouldn't have helped; you needed to soothe their physical pain and help them through their fright.

The same principles apply when learning to cope with rejection. Show your child how to move on. Remind them that the rejection isn't about them; it's about filling the role with the best actor for the part, and there are always criteria you know nothing about. When you give your child something concrete and positive to focus on, it can help still their mental chatter and show them how to let it go.

If your child is taking rejections hard and not bouncing back like they used to, it might be time to take a break from auditioning and focus on the fun aspects of the craft: acting classes and workshops for building skills and self-confidence in an environment that is rejection-free. Be sure to check in with yourself, too. Be sure you're not the one who's getting so wrapped up in the rejections that you're inflicting your disappointment on your child. How are *you* at letting it go and moving on? Watching your child get rejected can bring up your own stuff about rejection, and it's okay and indeed pragmatic to reach out to a life coach yourself to help you through.

 Life Lessons = Success

- No is just a word. Each rejection gets you closer to your next part.

- Learn to be friendly and supportive to other kids at auditions.

- When you are rejected it will hurt, but you will be able to move past it if you talk about your feelings and celebrate your courage in trying.

- Don't compare yourself to other people. Instead aim to always improve in your preparation and performance.

- Roles often go to actors who look the part, not necessarily to those with the most talent.

Chapter 11

Professional Training

Acting is not about being someone different.
It's finding the similarity in what is apparently different,
then finding myself in there.

— Meryl Streep

Along with her sister Lauren, Haley Fox co-owns three successful restaurants in New York City. Strangely, she can't cook! Haley credits her work as a child actor with her adult success. She shared, "I've behaved fearlessly throughout my whole life. Probably it's because I was not concerned about hearing the answer no. The attempts I've made in my career and my social life have always been with the belief that a possibility can always become a probability, and my being okay with it. I think about this a lot with my kids. I've tried to teach them to know and feel good about their strengths, but not try to hide what's not a strength. We all have different gifts to develop."

Haley started her acting career at age five. By the time she was eleven she was going to auditions on her own, fully responsible for showing up prepared and on time. When asked how her child-acting experience contributed to her adult success, Haley said, "It has been absolutely invaluable, especially the independence and responsibility. You feel very adult as a child actor. You feel like you're earning your way a bit. It's confidence-inspiring."

Today Haley is a busy mom who juggles lots of balls with her family and business responsibilities. She attributes her confidence and ability to continually grow to the lessons she learned while a young actress. When your child commits to acting, they commit to a continual process of learning. Successful young actors have a combination of natural charisma, passion, and skill. In this chapter I focus on how you can support your child in developing acting skills.

When I teach and guide my clients, I remind them that talent and passion are essential elements in an actor's life. Training is the glue that holds them together. Agent Ellen Gilbert added, "You have to pay your dues, you also have to learn, work hard, and put in the time and effort if you want to succeed as an actor."

It's not difficult for a child to understand that they need to improve their skills continually, just like an athlete is always practicing. You won't have to convince your child that attending an acting class, working with a coach, or attending theater camp is in their best interests. In fact, if they are truly passionate about acting, they will be bugging you for the chance to learn more.

I attended theater camp every summer, and adored it. In the beginning of my career as a young actress I was fortunate to apprentice at the Burt Reynolds Dinner Theater after college, where I watched great actors perform while I stood in the wings. Actors like Ned Beatty, Charles Durning, and Martin Sheen all did what they do best – act honestly, effortlessly, and powerfully, with material that helped them achieve that. I learned that I, too, could be great with good material, other good actors to play off of, and finding the truth in what I was saying and doing. I was excited to learn new acting techniques. Your child will be excited, too. If not, have a conversation with them about their passion to see if it's waning.

Learning Opportunities

There are three primary pathways I use to train child actors:

1. **Weekly group classes:** It is consistency and repetition of ongoing work that allows an actor to grow. Weekly classes help build a foundation that is essential for young actors as they work with others. Besides providing a fun place to make friends, group classes reinforce acting basics like listening and reacting, and encourage tackling difficult material. Start with an ongoing age-appropriate class. I like to keep my classes small to ensure personalized attention. Ask to audit a class to make sure it is the right fit for your child. Continuous classes are an investment in your child's artistic future that reap rewards in all aspects of their life.

2. **Workshops:** Audition workshops, musical theater boot camps, and one-day on-camera classes provide performers with an intensive experience devoted to improving a particular area of performance. What I find most valuable about workshops is that the environment pushes a performer to bring their A-game to a group of strangers. Workshops hone a specific skill, usually taught by an expert in a certain field both as a refresher and an opportunity to learn tools. Workshops are not a substitute for ongoing training. Like spicing up your exercise routine, workshops are a good setting for flexing certain performance muscles.

3. **Private coaching:** I spend many hours of my week coaching young actors privately in person and via Skype. The main benefit is they have my undivided attention. One-on-one coaching offers a personalized environment in which a young performer can feel safe and free to express themselves while being propelled to reach personal heights. A private coach becomes familiar with your performer, understands their strengths, and knows how to improve on their weaknesses.

Regular private coaching is essential for developing specific skills that can be lost in group classes. I highly recommend private coaching for professional children and children who frequent auditions. It is a crucial piece of a child's professional growth.

While each type of training has specific benefits, a combination of all three is best for a young performer. The mix of different acting environments ensures that your child becomes a well-rounded performer with diverse skills.

Improvisation Training

I believe that every young actor should also train in improvisation. Recently I heard from a former student of mine, Harvard professor Jacob Barandes, who said, "I learned a lot from your improv classes, and I find myself using those skills all the time when I teach."

Mastering improvisational skills tends to be wildly underrated. When parents have the option of choosing acting classes for young performers, improvisation usually falls to the bottom of the list, yet applying these skills reaches far beyond the world of acting. Improv training provides a competitive edge that leads to success in many important areas of life.

Children need to play. Improvisation fuels the imagination and helps them explore creativity. Working without a script, learning to work spontaneously, connecting with their instincts, and getting in tune with others promote creative growth for a young performer. Students who study improvisation with me find themselves hooked on it. They learn to conquer their fears, work collaboratively, laugh, and, most important, have fun.

Improvisation helps build a strong foundation. Acting classes for young performers focus on building a foundation for understanding the craft. Actors learn to dissect and understand scripts and characters, listen to their partners, and make important choices that are in line with character objectives. Improvisation provides an excellent way to apply these skills and expand them through practice.

The device used most often in improv is "Yes, and..." It means that you say "Yes" to anything thrown at you by your partner in a scene, then start your contribution with "and..." It is not enough to say yes to what your partner is doing in a scene; you must say, "Yes your hair looks great today, Jessica, and I hear you were voted homecoming queen!" It's important to add information to the scene to keep moving forward. Listening and responding appropriately are important skills to master in life. Doing so creatively brings joy and passion to what can otherwise be a structured and restrictive daily routine.

Improv is also great preparation for auditions. Actors need to be versatile and ready for anything thrown their way. It's important for casting directors to find out whether a child can take direction and adapt to any change that might occur with a script or while on set. Your child might be given a new script during the audition or be asked to read for a different role. If your child wants to succeed in a cold-read, they have to be able to trust their instincts with the material and live in the moment with confidence. In an audition for a commercial they might be asked to talk to a can of soup as if it's their best friend. While many actors might choke under this kind of pressure, if your child has improv experience they've done far sillier things. They will be able to say yes to that request and make the audition memorable to the casting director.

Improv training has so many benefits for young actors in developing both acting skills and life skills. Later in life, at a sales meeting or teacher's conference, or when leading a team, they will be able to think on their feet and speak with confidence. Consider it an essential part of your child's development.

Training for Very Young Children

If you are considering professional acting for your preschooler or five-, six-, or seven-year-old child, remember to encourage play and keep it fun. I do not push formal training on very young actors. Many young children, even those in the business, thrive without any training whatsoever. Young children can simply be allowed to let their natural abilities and personalities shine.

Nothing is more natural for most young children than dressing up and performing for adoring and encouraging adults. If you have an outgoing young child with imagination and a passion for performing, you can support their growth in these ways:

- Encourage them to use their imagination. Imitating characters, both real and imaginary, promotes healthy development and strengthens observation and imagination skills. It also helps deepen their understanding of other people in stories and life. This age-appropriate way to relate to characters serves the budding young actor especially well when transformed into sustained improvisation and dramatic play. I recommend that play of this type be a staple of family activities and downtime, to nurture young dramatic talent and desire.

- Encourage your child to sing with movement, play games that incorporate pitch, create emotional connections to all types of music, and learn musical concepts and vocabulary while playing. Parents can do this at home or in group classes. However, in the case of young children who already sing in numerous community productions and professional venues, it's worthwhile to seek a professional consultation. Master vocal teacher Badiene Magaziner has seen children as young as eight years old who already showed signs of vocal damage. Though some vocal teachers will not work with students before puberty, Magaziner believes, "It is crucial to have a solid technique that builds the head voice and teaches [children] how to mix properly so that they can grow up to have long careers!"

- Play lots of games. Think of games as the "Swiss Army knife" of training for young actors: there is a tool to develop just about every acting skill. Structured family games such as Kids on Stage, Pictionary, and other imaginative play should make up the largest part of every young child actor's training.

Private coaching might be appropriate for a very young actor if they are actively auditioning or performing and beginning to work with scripts. Skilled acting coaches for very young children create focus and structure while nurturing natural strengths and discouraging overacting. I include parents in the coaching process for very young children so that we work as a team to create a positive and healthy experience.

Where to Begin

If your child is just starting their acting career, look for workshops and acting classes in your local community. If they are musically inclined, voice lessons are helpful. Many young artists also participate in dance or other physical activities to learn how to use their bodies effectively.

Encourage your child to watch great performances, both live and on screen. Expose them to great acting by taking them to the theater and providing access to quality television and film performances. Encourage them to watch classics, period pieces, children's programming, and a variety of age-appropriate material. Consider tickets to plays for gifts, or plan a family vacation that includes Broadway shows.

How to Select the Right Acting Coach

Working with an individual acting coach can be a critical source of training and support. The success of a performer comes from their training, motivation, and passion. Just as in the Olympics, a qualified coach can make a significant difference in your child's training and ability to succeed.

Acting coaches are experts in enhancing performance skills. They are well trained, skilled, and know about the industry. Your child can work with an acting coach in person or via Skype. I work from New York with many actors across the country using Skype. It's not necessary to live in New York or Los Angeles to find a great coach for your young performer. I have two clients in Florida. We've worked exclusively on Skype for all of their training. One recently booked a role in the national touring company of *Annie*. The other just landed a role in a Nickelodeon television series.

There are many mature themes that arise while performing – topics that kids have never been exposed to. An experienced acting coach knows how to help children cope with adult themes in a sensitive and non-threatening way. I am currently coaching a nine-year-old working actress who has appeared in numerous roles on stage and in film. She is smart beyond her years, but still a young girl. While we were working on an audition scene for an upcoming Broadway show, her character had to ask the dad what an urn with ashes in it was. He responds, "something to remember your mom," meaning her cremated ashes. She had never heard of the word *cremated* and had no idea what it meant. I had to be the one to teach her about cremation and death to help her prepare for the audition.

Your child will benefit from coaching if you select a qualified and professional coach whom you trust. Trust is important because acting is such a personal business. You and your child must trust your acting coach to create a safe environment for growth. The best way to find a coach you can trust is to evaluate their professional etiquette, experience, and ethical standards.

Acting coaches can hang up a shingle without a teaching license or certification. They may be skilled, creative, well trained, and even a genius, but how moral and ethical are they? My students come to rely on me as a confidant and mentor as they bare their souls and become vulnerable. They speak their truths, insecurities, and fears while they dig within to learn who they are and how that relates to the characters they portray. It's deep work and requires me to be careful with their emotional growth.

Students often ask me for guidance and advice. They also share their excitement and joy when they are being considered for a role or book a job. The first thing they say is, "You're not going to tell anyone, right?" Confidentiality is important for production, and it is equally important in relationships. An eight-year-old student of mine booked a job, and when I asked him what it was, he replied, "I can't tell you because I signed a non-disclosure." He then coyly asked, "Mom, what does that mean?" Recently a student brought me a new monologue and made me swear I wouldn't give it to anyone else. They trust me to maintain their privacy and to coach them to their very best level of performance.

Before committing to a coach, do your homework. There is no union or legal sanction governing performance coaches, so ask around for recommendations, check them out on the web, read testimonials, and trust your gut. You know your child best. If you feel that something is off in the relationship between your child and an acting coach, trust that feeling and explore other options.

When you are looking for a trustworthy acting coach for your child, consider characteristics and behaviors that point to a high level of professionalism that will create safety for your child. Does the coach:

- Gossip?
- Accurately identify their coaching qualifications, expertise, and experience?
- Recognize personal issues that could interfere with their coaching performance?
- Report research with competency and honesty?

- Avoid conflicts of interest?
- Take personal or monetary advantage of a client?
- Give misleading information or advice?
- Become sexually intimate with clients?
- Respect a client's right to terminate coaching, and not blacklist them?
- Maintain the strictest level of confidentiality?

When you and your child come to trust the acting coach, fear and anxiety are no longer in the way and your young actor can open up and do their best work. Developing the art of performance requires much from a young actor. A trustworthy, ethical, and experienced coach makes a big impact on that process.

Summer Camp Options

As your child progresses they will want more advanced training. Summer camp can become the highlight of your child's year. All I wanted to do as a child actress was eat, breathe, and live theater. For me that meant spending my summer doing show after show after show at camp. I wanted to be with kids who "got" me. I didn't hang around with the popular crowd or the intellectuals. My social comfort zone was with the theater geeks. I couldn't imagine a better way to spend eight weeks of my summer than fitting in and doing what I loved. As an adult I also spent my summers at theater camps directing and teaching, so I have some experience with these programs that might be of interest to you.

I was only seven years old when I went to a sleep-away camp for eight full weeks. I was very independent, and loved it, but your child might not be as independent at that age.

Today there is a wide variety of theater camp options ranging from day camps to two to eight weeks of overnight camp. If your child does not like to be away from you and might get homesick, day camp is the perfect solution for now. Overnight camp teaches your child independence and responsibility while fostering close-knit, lifelong relationships with other young performers. Both offer the same kinds of activities with classes in acting, voice, dance, and rehearsing and putting on a show.

Do your research to find the right camp for your child. Here are some sleep-away options for your young performer:

- **Stagedoor Manor Performing Arts Training Center** in Loch Sheldrake, New York, focuses only on theater arts. Although there is an outside pool, there are no sports or fine-arts programs. Their goal is education, performance, and community. They validate kids' passions and encourage them to build relationships with other kids like themselves doing what they love – theater! Agents, managers, and casting directors love to visit this camp in the summer to scout new talent.

- **Frenchwoods Festival of the Performing Arts** in upstate New York is another wonderful sleep-away camp that places a strong emphasis on the performing arts. It offers a wide variety of programs in everything from circus to art to cooking. Industry pros also visit this camp in hopes of discovering the next big star.

- **Long Lake Camp for the Arts** in the Adirondacks is in a spectacular mountain setting and offers a complete non-competitive camping experience in addition to performing-arts experiences. It has a different vibe in that campers choose daily what they would like to do, mixing theater arts with traditional camping experiences.

- **Interlochen Arts Camp**, located in beautiful northwestern Michigan, offers one- to six-week summer programs for grades three through twelve. This is an audition-based program with scholarships available. It is a large program, with 2,500 students from all over the world who come to study music, theater, visual arts, creative writing, motion picture arts, and dance. What is unique about this program is not just the location, but that artists from all over the world collaborate and support each other.

Talk with your child to find out what kind of summer camp experience most excites them, and look for one that meets those needs. Be aware that camps vary in size. With about 290 campers, the staff at Stagedoor knows everyone by name. Even smaller, Long Lake has 250 campers per session with a staff of 160. Interlochen has about 350 students in the theater-arts program. Frenchwoods can have upwards of 800 campers in various programs. When you are interviewing camp personnel, ask how many campers there are in each bunkhouse and the total number in the community. Only you know if your child will do better in a smaller or larger camp community.

Sleep-away camp used to be affordable. At today's price tag of $3,000 to $5,000 for a three-and-a-half-week session, some camps have become cost prohibitive for many people. Here's the truth: they are all expensive! And here's a secret tip: everything is negotiable. Ask about scholarships. Some camps want and need more boys, and offer a discount or even a free ride for boys in some cases. If you don't ask, you will never know what might be available.

Day programs

I run one-week programs in the summer in New York City, giving kids an intensive experience in musical theater and on-camera training. Many of my colleagues in New York and Los Angeles run similar programs. If sleep-away camp is not for your child or doesn't fit into your budget, check out local day programs.

As we all know, the school year can be stressful for kids, especially young working actors who carry the burden of both work and school. Summer camp should be fun, so find a camp that meets the needs of your child and provides training that will be fun.

 Life Lessons = Success

- Confidence comes from competence. Competence comes from continued learning and growth.
- The more you train and practice, the better you become.
- When you want to master a skill, ask an expert to guide you.
- Learn improvisation skills to improve your confidence and creativity.
- Take responsibility for your success and your growth.

Chapter 12

Self-Taped Auditions

*The first step to a better audition is to give up character
and use yourself.*

— Michael Shurtleff

You met Noah Fleiss in chapter 9. Noah's thirty-year acting career in films and television and on stage began when he was seven years old. I asked Noah about some of the benefits he gained from becoming a child actor. He shared, "First of all I would say the benefits outweigh the cost by a landslide. The first thing was learning social skills at an early age. Having to be on set and be around adults for many hours a day, and being asked to show up as an adult ready to perform, helped give me an emotional awareness that a lot of kids don't have. Secondly, I definitely think that having been a child actor instilled in me a really strong work ethic, a sense of diligence. Working an eight-hour day at ten years old lays the groundwork for someone who is going to give it his all. I couldn't just say, 'I'm too tired, I can't film the rest of the day,' when there's lots of money riding on the production and the schedule."

Noah has seen many changes in the industry over the years, especially in the audition process. "One thing that stands out is the self-tape new phenomenon. I don't tape with casting directors as much as I used to. Now I do many first auditions at home with my fiancée and my cell phone."

Casting directors and college drama admissions teams are increasingly using video auditions to screen young actors. Video auditions reduce travel time and expense and make the first-audition process more efficient for everyone.

If you have a smart phone or camera with video recording capability, you can help your child successfully create video auditions at home. Your camera or phone should be able to record clearly with excellent sound quality. Use an external microphone for the actor's voice to tip the sound balance in their favor. Microphones can be purchased for as little as $10 each and are well worth it. Not only do you get more clarity, but mics with sensitivity control have the flexibility to make great recordings in quiet and chaotic settings alike.

Use a tripod so that the video is steady. Film in a quiet room with a blank wall behind your child. Ensure that the room is well lit so their face can be clearly seen. Position the camera to show them from the shoulders up.

It's important to rehearse well and do several practice videos. When I show students playback of themselves rehearsing, they cringe, but it provides essential information about how they appear to an audience and shows what to improve on. Kids can discover unconscious habits like blinking, licking their lips, raising their eyebrows, and playing with their hair and clothes. They see how the camera picks up the slightest movements and sounds, which leads to the biggest difference between working on camera versus the stage: subtlety. Young actors who have only worked on stage need to learn how to tone down their facial expressions, body movements, and voice for the camera. The only way to master these things is to keep practicing on camera.

Your child should memorize the script for the video. When an actor looks down at their notes, their face disappears from the camera and we just see the top of their head. Although adult actors can be adept at working with the script in hand, children get easily distracted by it and are not able to remain present and listen. An actor's emotional life exists in their eyes, so it's important to know the dialogue by heart so they can stay present in the scene, focus on their partner, and respond to directions.

Parents are often very concerned about their child's clothing and hair. I've seen parents mess with their child's hair to the point of making the child crazy. It's important that your child is relaxed during the taping. Let them select something that fits the character without wearing a costume. For example, if the character is down and out, messy hair and clothing would be appropriate. Instead of obsessing about the perfect outfit or hairstyle, focus on helping your child connect to the character in appearance and interpretation of the material.

Tips for Reading with Child Actors on Video

When taping your child's audition, you can read all the other parts. You don't have to be a trained actor to be a good reading partner for your child. Even if you have acting talent, while reading with your child remember to keep the focus on them. In the supporting role of "great reading partner" for your child, the following tips will help you help your young performer shine:

- **Stand or sit off screen.** You should not be seen on camera, so position yourself right next to the camera. Unless directed otherwise, sit or stand where your child can look at you while speaking instead of appearing to address the camera. They should speak to and connect with you, so stay at their eye level.

- **Speak softly so you don't steal the focus.** It's your child's audition, not yours. Since you are positioned closest to the camera, your voice will sound louder than your child's unless you continually remind yourself to speak softly. You are not co-starring in this scene, but rather providing a framework that supports your child's purposes.

- **Read fluently.** Practice your lines. The more familiar you are with the script and lines, the more effectively you can support your partner. You are there to help your child do the best job they can, so invest the time needed to prepare. Your pace is important, especially in comedy, so you also need to practice the timing. If you read too slowly or too quickly it can throw your child off and kill the humor. Ask for help if you are unsure of the best pace or timing. If another family member or friend has better acting or comedy skills than you do and offers the time, allow them to do the readings with your child. Remember, this is not about you, and it is important that your child has a competent reading partner.

- **Read all the other parts, skipping the stage directions.** One person reads for all the characters in the scene. Having additional people play other parts is confusing and unnecessary. Keep in mind that stage directions are there for information only. Make sure you and your child understand the stage directions, but stick to the usual protocol and do not read stage directions aloud on camera.

- **Don't judge or criticize.** This is not the time to offer advice on your child's performance. An actor should not be distracted by concerns of the reader's perceptions during this process. If you have an idea or healthy suggestion to offer, feel free to take notes for discussion at a later time, as long as jotting down your thoughts doesn't interfere with the flow of the reading. While reading, your focus needs to stay on playing the character(s) and providing the support your child needs.

- **Keep it fun!** This is your child's dream, and you are there to support them. If they get stressed or feel criticized, they will not be able to do their best.

There is pressure to get the video right for a great role or to meet a college application deadline. Use that pressure as motivation to prepare well, not to demand perfection. Natural performances are good performances. Kids mess up; expect them to do just that. Sometimes the best moments are the mistakes.

It's frustrating to shoot and reshoot the same material with little to show for the effort. Stress begins when actors believe that their next big break relies on a perfect video submission. There is no such thing as perfect. Casting directors look for "real" young actors. Colleges look for potential, connection, and emotional truth. Perfection is not on anyone's list. If your imperfect video suggests that your child might have what they're looking for, your child will, in all likelihood, get a callback. Remember that casting directors are seeking specific physical characteristics as well as talent. College faculty also consider factors beyond a student's control, such as a balance of male to female students and a diverse student body. More takes do not always equate to a better video. The more hours spent on one video, the more tired the actor gets and the more forced and less natural it becomes.

Be aware of what you can and can't control, and let go of the outcome. You can control the level of preparation, but not whether your child is selected for a part. As my colleague, television and film casting director Matthew Maisto, CSA, said, "Only one person gets the role! Don't make it personal; most actors auditioning aren't going to get the job. Unlike most businesses, our industry is mainly subjective regarding decision making. No grading system in casting means there's no way for an actor to understand what they could have done 'better' to change the outcome. Most of the time the answer is you just weren't *it*. Simply put, another actor was more right for the role. Keep in mind that auditioning for a role in a film, on TV, or a play is not a competition with judges and a score card to determine who's the most talented. Usually, we are not looking for the best actor, but rather the right actor. Many factors inform which actor is seen as the most right for a role. Presence and personality are often just as important as skill and natural talent."

Uploading the Video

Learn how to use iMovie or Windows Media Player for uploading and editing if necessary. Look at a YouTube video or hire a high school student who knows how to do this.

The file will be too large to email, so once you have successfully uploaded the file, use Dropbox, We Transfer, or Hightail to send it to your agent or manager. If sending directly to the casting director, follow their instructions about how to upload videos to their preferred location.

Does My Child Need an Acting Coach?

There are times when working with an acting coach, especially on video auditions, can be useful. An experienced acting coach can help a young actor make choices about how to approach the script, and point out bad habits such as distracting facial expressions or vocal issues that might get in the way of a great audition. It is often easier for a young actor to receive performance feedback from a coach than from a parent. If they already have an acting coach, ask your child if they feel confident with the material or if working with their coach would give them the upper hand. We can sometimes underestimate our children. They often know what they need.

I spoke with talent agent Natasha Matallana Marken, President of Take 3 Talent Agency in New York. She said, "In my previous experience, casting has frowned upon 'over-coached' kids and preferred kids with a natural overall approach. But today, it seems that around ages seven or eight, there's a need for coaching as the material gets a bit more difficult. I find coaching helps a young actor understand the material, not just regurgitate the lines. If parents don't have the ability to work with their child, or other distractions present themselves, I recommend seeking out a professional acting coach who can properly rehearse and teach in a conventional, or sometimes unconventional instructional setting."

With the insurgence of the "self-tape" phenomenon, some coaches provide an excellent combination of training for the actor and the ability to produce quality self-tapes, as they usually have high-end professional cameras, lighting kits, backdrops, etc., and, more important, they know what the casting director wants to see. A good self-tape takes a lot of skill.

However, sometimes casting directors specify that a child must not be coached for an audition. If that's the case, do not bring in a coach for that audition.

If your child does not have an acting coach yet, use these three questions to determine if they need one:

1. **How difficult is the material?** Maybe it's an emotional scene in which the actor has to cry or get angry. Maybe the character is blind or has a disability. Maybe it's a period piece or a dialect is required. Sketch comedy and improvisation skills might be necessary. Your child would benefit by working with a coach for any of these reasons. However, if the audition involves one or two lines and the performer just needs to be natural and be themselves, save your money.

2. **Does your child need a boost of confidence?** In addition to working on skills with the young actor, a good coach is also a cheerleader and one of your child's biggest fans. Of course you're rooting for your child, but according to my child, what I say doesn't count because "parents always say nice things." Sound like any child you know?

3. **Has it been a while since your child got a callback?** Perhaps their skills are rusty. Now may be a good time to check in with a coach. Brushing up on improvisation, acting, and on-camera and audition techniques might be just what is needed to put your young actor back on the map.

Video auditioning will surely become even more prevalent in the future. Helping your young actor get comfortable with being taped at home is a worthwhile investment of your time and energy. Consider adding a professional acting coach to your child's success team to consult on complicated video auditions as needed, but your child should not look coached; you should not "see" the technique or process; they must remain real and natural, and demonstrate an understanding of the character and the material.

 Life Lessons = Success

- Acting is a business. When you are cast, you are expected to show up and do the work just as an adult would.

- Learning to speak clearly and confidently helps you throughout your entire life.

- All people have hidden habits that only show up on camera. While you may not like how you look or sound on video, you will gain valuable information for improving your skills.

- Reading scripts thoroughly and carefully prepares you for reading important documents later in life.

- Understanding and following instructions leads to success.

Chapter 13

Supporting Your Child's Education

*There's nothing more boring than unintelligent actors,
because all they have to talk about is themselves and
acting. There have to be other things.*

—Tim Robbins

A student of mine, Caleb McLaughlin, started acting in his local community theater at age seven. By age ten he was appearing on Broadway in *The Lion King*. Today fifteen-year-old Caleb is in a leading role in the award-winning television series *Stranger Things*. I asked Caleb how he manages his responsibilities in *Stranger Things* along with his school. He said, "Nothing has changed. I've always had the mindset to work hard, stay focused, and be responsible for learning lines without my parents telling me." His mother, April McLaughlin, added, "School is VERY important to Caleb. School is his number one priority. It's not unusual to find Caleb doing school on the weekends or at night after a full day of filming. It's important for Caleb to excel in school."

While your child is busy learning how to be an entertainer, they must still attend to their basic educational requirements. In this chapter I provide a broad overview of how production companies and parents support young actors' traditional educational requirements. It is important to remember that educational requirements vary widely. Each school district and state has laws and expectations for children at each grade level. Beyond what I provide in this chapter, it's imperative to work with your child's local school to understand the requirements and to create a cooperative relationship that will help your child manage the demands of being a working actor and a student.

Alan Simon is a former actor who founded On Location Education in the early 1980s to support the educational needs of children appearing on Broadway. For thirty years On Location Education has provided educational services on theater, television, and film sets around the nation, as well as private education for actors who travel frequently or need a unique educational environment. It has become the premier provider in the nation for productions that feature children. I am very grateful for Alan's consultation on this chapter. For additional information visit Alan's website at www.OnLocationEducation.com.

In the 1980s the Screen Actors Guild created a national prototype for working with young actors that covered both the number of hours that could be worked each day and guidelines for providing on-set tutoring for each child. Over the years these guidelines were influenced by state labor laws, and further revisions were made. According to SAG-AFTRA, if a minor is guaranteed three or more consecutive days of employment, the production company is responsible for providing them with a tutor. All productions are required to provide a clean, well-lit, quiet workspace for children. The producer provides schooling equipment and supplies. However, the minor's parent or guardian must, if permitted by the child's regular school, secure school assignments and books for use at the place of employment. Costs associated with on-set education are the responsibility of the production company.

Complex rehearsal and filming schedules can make this requirement challenging. On some days the required three hours of education might be broken up into shorter increments. Another challenge is that education is regulated by both the curriculum requirements of the child's local school district and the laws of the state where the production is being created. So if there are five children on a movie set, they might use five different textbooks for each subject and be required to study state history from five different states. There is a ratio of one teacher for each ten children, so on-site classrooms have the feel of a one-room school with everyone working on individual lessons.

Work Permits

All performers under the age of eighteen or who have not yet graduated from high school are required by law to obtain a free Child Performer Permit. The entertainment industry is not covered by the Federal Labor Standards Act (FLSA), thus the reason for state-by-state work permits.

- For work permits in California, apply at www.dir.ca.gov/DLSE/OnlinePermits.htm.
- For work permits in New York, apply at https://www.labor.ny.gov/secure/ChildPerformer/welcome.html.
- If your child is working in another state, google "Child Actor Work Permit" and the state in question.

Child Performer Permits ensure that working child actors are educated appropriately and that any earnings are protected. Each state has its guidelines for both finances and schooling. Most states require the signature of an official from the child's school on the permit application. New York and California require that earnings are kept in a trust. It is the parent's responsibility to apply for the work permit, renew it regularly, and provide copies to each employer.

Educational expectations vary widely. For example, if a child from California is filming a movie in the state of New York, they are bound by California educational law rather than New York law because of the way California education law is written. Each school district has its own requirements for attendance and grade-level competencies.

New York and California have some of the most comprehensive educational laws for professional children to ensure that schooling is not neglected. In New York, a letter from your school district confirming your child is in good standing with your school, signed by the principal or the district supervisor, is required in order to obtain a work permit. California requires a letter grade of C or higher in every subject before granting a work permit to a child. It is crucial for your child to maintain academic excellence.

"Getting a grade of C gets you a permit, but being a good student requires more than just eking by," said Alan Simon. "A child should be able to meet the home school's requirements, with a thorough understanding of his or her assignments, and a willingness to work them through with the tutor, wherever the location may be on a given day. Schooling on set is a discipline, just like playing a character is."

It can be challenging for parents to understand all the different regulations and expectations for their child actors. These steps will help you:

1. Consult the SAG-AFTRA union office that covers your state.

2. Apply for a Child Performer Permit from the required state. This permit is free but might require educational, financial, and health-related documentation to ensure the safety of your child.

3. Form a positive working relationship with your child's teacher, guidance counselor, and local principal.

4. Talk with other parents of working actors about their experiences.

Alan Simon reminds us of the importance of keeping an open mind and understanding the local school's point of view. Many local schools are not accustomed to serving students who are employed as actors, though they understand how to work with children who are ill and miss a lot of school or need to travel for athletic events. Public schools are funded based on attendance, so when your child is absent for an extended period your local school loses funding as well as the opportunity to educate. While landing a role is a wonderful thing for your child, it can create a lot of hassles and challenges for their school. You can even be charged with truancy if things get stressed between you and the local district. So start out on the right foot with your school by being open and cooperative.

It is also important to understand the point of view of the production company, which is required to provide a certain number of on-site education hours; however, it is not required to replicate the experience your child would have at their school. For instance, it won't provide laboratory facilities for studying biology, chemistry, etc. Your child is a member of a cast, not the only actor the production company needs to consider. You will occasionally have input into the selection of your child's on-site teacher, but not often.

If your child has special needs through an Individual Education Plan, inform the casting director of that before accepting a role so that the production company is aware of any special educational requirements. For example, if your child requires support services during the school day, the production company needs to know that before hiring your child to ensure it can meet their needs. Your child's agent or manager should handle those negotiations for you.

Finally, have realistic expectations of your child. If they are busy auditioning and working as an actor, is it realistic to expect a 4.0 grade point average? For very bright children that expectation is perfectly realistic; for those less academically gifted it is not.

Educational Options

Some parents decide that working with the local public or private school is too difficult when their child is cast in a tour or in a role that will last a long time. They opt for homeschooling or enrolling in a charter school that focuses on the arts or a private educational institution that can supplement on-set educational services. Some working teen actors take the GED so that they can focus on acting. Others are college bound and want to ensure that they are well prepared for the SAT and ACT examinations as well as able to meet university admission requirements.

Homeschooling may sound like an easy option, but it can be a difficult balancing act when a parent takes on the role of teacher on top of being the career administrator. It's a decision that only you and your family can make based on the needs of your child. On this topic, Alan Simon said, "The parent has the right to homeschool the child if they want to, but they should think very carefully if that is their strength. It seems easier to homeschool when your child is elementary school-aged, but as they get older and the work becomes more challenging, the family may want to rethink their options." If you choose to homeschool your child, it is your job to show the state that your child is receiving a proper education as defined by your local school district.

Some families prefer to homeschool through a variety of programs, some independent, some religious, and some affiliated with universities and other institutions of learning. There are also many public *magnet schools* that support drama majors and working performers. Whatever you choose, make sure that your school of record will sign your child's work permit. Completion of satisfactory educational performance must be attested to by a recognized public, private, or homeschooling program for your child to legally work in at least forty of the fifty states.

Schools that are supportive of the working actor's lifestyle come in many forms. In addition to the School for Young Performers, there is the Professional Children's School in New York City. Shari Honig, Admissions Director, explains that Professional Children's School is an independent school for grades six through twelve with approximately 200 students. It's a college preparatory academic program. All the students at PCS are seriously pursuing the arts, entertainment, or athletics at a pre-professional or professional level. Students have scheduling flexibility when they need it in order to go to and prepare for auditions, performances, recitals, concerts, and competitions.

I asked Shari about the kinds of students who thrive at PCS. She shared, "Students who are as serious about their academics as they are about their pre-professional and professional pursuits thrive at PCS. We have a student population that comes from fourteen different states and about thirteen different countries. It's a school for students who are not looking for a lot of extracurricular activities because that's one thing we don't provide. We don't have sports teams or an after-school program. I think if a student can very proudly and confidently say, 'I am an actor,' or 'I am a dancer,' it's a good fit for them. We really help the students learn to advocate for themselves, work independently and find their intrinsic motivation, but I think a student who thinks it's just going to be an easy ride, will probably not do well at PCS."

It is important to be flexible and willing to explore the best educational options for your child. Ask a lot of questions of your local school district, state union representative, and production companies to ensure you understand all the components and educational requirements.

Homework Tips

Going to school while attending auditions and working can be a heavy burden for anyone, especially a child or teenager. Here are some tips to help you manage the scheduling demands of your busy young performer:

- **Be sure your child gets enough rest.** Not only can sleep deprivation lead to poor school and acting performance, but it can also compromise your child's immune system, resulting in allergies or other sickness. If your child starts to miss school due to illness, playing catch up will just add more stress and make fulfilling their acting obligations extremely difficult.

- **Ensure your child is eating a healthy, balanced diet.** Yes, this is easier said than done. I have kids of my own, and they like sweets. When they are filled with sugar and carbs, they are lethargic, moody, and not at the top of their game. The next time your child needs a pick-me-up, substitute a protein bar for that Snickers bar.

- **Maintain good communication with the school and teachers.** Consulting with the school in advance is absolutely a key element to creating a supportive school environment and helping your child stay on top of their academics.

- **Develop a good routine.** Sticking to a regular schedule and routine helps balance the work and school load. The problem is that show business does *not* follow a schedule. For the working child actor there are hold days, reshoots, matinee performances, and unexpected changes in the schedule. Create a good routine and help your child learn to be flexible on those days when the regular routine needs to be altered.

- **Keep a long-range view.** While it can be tempting to focus on your child's current successes, remember that their education is important for their whole life whether or not they continue to act. Don't short-change their education.

Many of my students go on to do great work in college and graduate school. You and your child do not need to sacrifice academic success for performing. Succeeding at both is possible.

 Life Lessons = Success

- Education is important. Keeping up with your school work is required, and the industry looks for smart actors.

- You can learn to balance your time and attention to fulfill all of your responsibilities.

- Life requires you to set priorities and make some sacrifices to get what you really want.

- Laws govern most workplaces. You are responsible for knowing workplace expectations.

- Success in acting, as well as in education, requires discipline and dedication.

Chapter 14

The Role of Parents

*When you start so young working, you build a hunger
for acting, working, and a busy life.*
— Bonnie Wright

Lenore Riegel knows what it's like to be the parent of a working child actor. Her children, Sam and Eden, entered show business at a young age and today are adult actors. Sam and Eden were preforming regularly in their local community theater in Virginia when the national touring company of *Les Miserables* held an open call for local kids. Sam spent two-and-a-quarter years and Eden more than three years in *Les Miserables*. Then Sam and Eden settled in New York and went on to play many roles in films, voice-over work, television, and theater. Eden won an Emmy for her role as Bianca in *All My Children*. Sam works for Disney, DreamWorks, and Nickelodeon as a voice-over director and does voice work himself.

At the time the children were cast in the touring company of *Les Miserables*, Lenore owned a successful business and was not able to go on the road with them, so her mother accompanied the children on tour. She later moved to New York so that the children could continue working and attend the Professional Children's School.

Lenore has much advice to share with parents of young actors. First, she believes that your primary job is to be a parent, not an acting coach. She shared:

> My children worked very hard. They loved it, but it was not easy. My job was to be kind of a personal assistant, a facilitator. I made sure that they could do what they did because I took care of all the details. I ordered the headshots and updated their resumes. I found out where the audition was and I drove them there. I made sure they had their food, their school work and made a good home for them. The agent should do what the agent does best, and the manager should do what the manager does best. The children should do what they do best. The mother should be a mother and the father a father. When you are the mother of the child who is performing every day – and this could be in chess or gymnastics or soccer, it doesn't have to be theater – it's a huge sacrifice on the part of the parents financially and in time. I'm not saying it's easy. It's a big deal for parents. You give up a lot, but the children shouldn't see that. What they should be seeing is, "That's my mom, she lets me do what I want to do best." That was what I strove to do.

Communication was crucial. Lenore's children asked her not to review scripts with them or even attend their opening nights. They wanted to concentrate on their acting and not on her reactions. It is a tribute to the strength of their relationships that they were able to have these kinds of conversations. Eden said in such a sweet way, "I don't want you to come to my opening nights because I love you so much. I would probably feel a little less certain about what I was doing with my character. I will let you know when I have finished my work, and then you can come, and you can say whatever you want because by that time I will know what I want to do."

The Riegel children learned many life lessons from their acting careers. One of the most important was responsibility to the other cast members. Lenore remembered, "The children were treated as theater professionals at a young age. They were not lesser. They were up there on the stage, and they had to perform as if they were an adult performer. They didn't get any slack for being young. They still had to sing on key. They had to meet their mark. They had to be backstage. They had to come on when they were supposed to. There's a lot of responsibility on the children. That I think is a good thing. In no other way are you ever treated as a child with the respect that adults get. You do in theater. They understood their importance as an equal partner. They knew they had to work their tail off to earn the respect. They knew that they had to be a professional. They were a part of the success of the show."

As a former teacher, Lenore worked hard to ensure that both Sam and Eden graduated from high school and went to college. It was challenging, as they were both working so much. Eden didn't attend a full week of traditional school during a four-year period due to her travel schedule, yet she was very dedicated to her studies and was accepted at Harvard. Sam graduated from the University of Virginia.

When I asked Lenore if she had any advice for other parents, she stated, "I believe it is a parent's job to expose the children to enough so that they can find what it is that makes them happy. It might be chess; it might be bicycling; it might be needlepoint. It is your job as a parent to provide opportunities. My kids were in scouts, sports, and played a musical instrument. It wasn't just all theater. It was one of the things they did. Little by little you could see that that's where their interest lay. Acting is a great life if your children love it and if you are willing to commit to them reaching their dream. It can be a wonderful life for the parent too, but on a daily basis, you have to make sure it's centered on the child's dream. It doesn't become your dream. It's very easy for you to buy into it.

I've had times when I've been a little too involved emotionally, put too much of myself into their careers. You do have to hold back."

Karine Schnapp agrees: "Parents must realize that this is their child's life, not yours. You are there, as a parent, to provide the guardrails; you are their champion to help them get through the difficult times, the person to bounce ideas off of. However, a child actor has to eventually learn to develop their own opinion and point of view, and ensure they are not channeling your own."

Your role as a parent of a child actor is to parent them, protect them, and ensure they are given the nurturing and support required to work in a stressful business. You are their best advocate. No one else can parent your child as well as you can.

Being the parent of a young actor is both thrilling and challenging. There is a fine balance between supporting their career and trying to control it. I've observed some parents become too involved and stress their children so much that the joy goes out of acting. The parent-coach, sometimes known as the "stage mom," is an all too common occurrence in the world of young performers. Instead of leaving the lessons to the professionals, the parent-coach takes on the role of acting, voice, and dance teacher all in one stroke, and usually with no formal training. The entertainment industry is a tough one, especially for a child. You want to support your child, not lead them astray. Instead of being a parent-coach, think about becoming a parent-mentor instead.

I have seen countless young performers come to lessons with me already having "learned" their scene. They've practiced it with their parent beforehand, who has given them direction. Often parent-coaches instruct their children to practice in front of a mirror. The results are disastrous. How can a child explore their emotional connection to their scene partner if they're looking at themselves in a mirror? How can they stay focused on being in the moment when they are distracted by their reflection? When I see this, I usually have to spend hours deconstructing a child's bad habits, enabling them to get to the "truth" of their scene.

The over-coached child is a casting director's worst nightmare. Casting professionals can spot it in a second, and it usually ends with your child's resume in the "no" pile. They are looking for children who are unique, who have passions, who are real kids. Don't hinder your child's abilities by espousing your ideas. Instead, help your child by entrusting them to the care of skilled professionals.

It's also important to stay calm in the waiting room, which is one of the most stressful parts of an audition. Shoving last-minute tips and tricks down your child's throat – telling them to remember to smile and sit up straight, to not forget that line, or to look sad at the end of the scene – are all typical examples of the wrong kind of audition advice. While they are well intentioned, it is usually a recipe for an over-coached and stressed-out child. Instead, talk to them about their day, put their mind at ease, support them by reaffirming their abilities, and tell them to have fun. That's why they're doing this! Remind them of that passion while giving them confidence in their strengths.

The healthiest child actors come from families that provide lots of support. Here are some ways you can support your child's passion for acting without putting on pressure:

- **Encourage them to take control of their career.** There comes a time when they need to be the authority for their dreams. Encourage them to follow up with agents and look for audition opportunities. Talk about the kinds of roles they would like to play. Hands-on involvement is a great way for children to recognize that you value them as individuals.

- **Make sure photos and resumes are up to date.** Kids change and grow quickly! Remember that your child's photo is their calling card – the first thing people see when your child is being considered for a role.

- **Encourage your child to go outside of their comfort zone so they stay well-rounded.** Maybe your child is interested in marital arts or wants to audition for a role outside of their type. It's always remarkable what kids learn when put in a new environment. Kids with a wide variety of interests and skills are more appealing.

- **Help them create a list of goals.** Whether it's as big as mastering a difficult song or as simple as improving their posture during auditions, creating a list of goals offers a chance for your child to be candid with you about their career.

- **Creativity is everything for young artists.** Encourage your child to collaborate with others to create sketches. Collaboration is a skill that transcends all professions – plus, you never know if they'll come up with the next award-winning work! One of my clients, Ella Koski (Broadway's Young Cosette), and her dad started a YouTube channel called Broadway Bakes where Ella teaches people how to bake on video. The project gives Ella a wonderful outlet for her creativity and practice in front of the camera.

- **Eat dinner as a family.** From eating dinner in the car to eating while sitting in the audition waiting room, it can be hard to catch up as a family. Sometimes your spouse's career, your career, or your child's career is the sole focus of conversation, so take the time to appreciate your family for being your family and not professionals by eating together and sharing different aspects of your lives at the table.

- **Explore volunteer opportunities in the arts.** There are so many great organizations dedicated to bringing the arts to communities and spaces that need them most. Whether it's music therapy for the elderly or musical theater workshops in disadvantaged areas, volunteering is a remarkable way for your child to give back and learn about themselves.

- **Have a movie marathon!** Have a fun day with your child! Work can't be 100 percent of your relationship. Make some popcorn and enjoy watching movies with your family. It is a great learning tool to see your child's favorite actor in all types of works. Let them know you admire their role models and give them opportunities to be inspired!

- **Aim for a healthy balance for your child.** Though it takes real skills to perform at a high level, don't specialize in acting to the point of pushing all other activities aside. Find a balance that leaves room for religious education and activities, sports, the school yearbook committee, or whatever non-performance-related activities your family and child value. These events create opportunities for serious actors to form a broad range of relationships and skills that provide the life experiences they need to succeed both on and off the set.

- **Help your child maintain friendships to mitigate stress and so they can enjoy their childhood.** Being a child actor requires so much time and energy that friendships can fall by the wayside. Encourage your child to use free time to enjoy activities with friends. All work and no play is not healthy!

Red Flags to Watch For

Young actors and their parents can become burned out and overstressed. If your child is unusually cranky, having trouble with schoolwork, plagued with illness, or doesn't want to see friends, consider taking a break from acting for a short time. Encourage your child to try a new activity or sport and engage in activities that non-performing kids do. Have fun as a family as well. If you see signs of depression or become concerned that something is off kilter, consult your physician or a child psychologist.

Watch your stress level as well. It can be extremely discouraging for a parent to take their child from audition to audition and watch them be consistently rejected. Children are experts at reading their parents' emotions. If a child thinks they are a disappointment to their parents, they will not want to continue acting, even if it is their passion.

Your personal self-care is vitally important. Be sure to exercise, eat properly, and take the time to do things that make you happy. Being the parent of a child actor can be very stressful, especially if you have left your job and are traveling away from your spouse and other children. You need to stay healthy so you can support your child.

Few parents are prepared for the enormous commitment of a tour, Broadway show, film, or television series. The experience often comes with many delightful and difficult moments. It can be a wonderful investment of time, but financially draining. It is exhilarating to see a child blossom, but isolating to be apart from family and friends. A parent can gain a lifetime of precious memories, but be left physically exhausted. The key to success for both the parent and young actor is to prepare for the challenges, remain flexible and creative when solving problems, and stay organized. Here are some tips to make your experience as the parent of a working child actor a happy and successful one:

- **Know what you are getting into by speaking to the parents of other child actors in the show.** Every production has its unique challenges. For example, some production companies provide tutoring while others don't. Make a list of all the organizational, financial, and emotional challenges you are likely to encounter. This includes issues around marriage, raising other children, finances, housing, and employment, to name a few. For example, one parent I know deals with the close quarters of hotel rooms by booking suites. Another negotiated tutoring for her other child, whom she also takes on the road.

- **Hold family conferences.** The life of a working child actor affects every member of the family. Have a family discussion before accepting any offer. It is likely that siblings will have to be more independent, spouses will have to work harder and endure loneliness, and details of home life go unattended. Be specific with new responsibilities. Make sure everyone is on the same page and willing to accept the changes that go along with supporting a working actor. Don't forget that there will be expenses and challenges regarding your children who are not acting to ensure they get the attention they require.

- **Be realistic.** Once on set, on the road, or in a production, be flexible. You can't plan for everything. Some things cost more, take more time, or go undone. An extra plane ticket for a sibling who misses an on-the-road parent is often the cost of supporting a young actor's work.

- **Be organized.** Driving long hours, eating on the run, and sleep deprivation are often part of the job. Your daily routine of staying healthy – including cooking healthy meals and exercising – will now be compromised unless you are well organized. Keep a regular schedule to ensure you remain focused. Do research to plan for the next stop on tour. Knowing that the grocery store is only a block from your hotel can make all the difference when you are checking in late and have to prepare for the next day.

- **Keep your marriage healthy.** Nothing beats sitting with your spouse and watching your child happily perform; however, there will be times when you and your partner are separated for long periods. Make your marriage a priority. Be prepared for unanticipated stresses from employment issues, child-rearing, and separation. It is often very helpful to have a trusted family member take over the chaperoning duties for a bit while parents get together to recharge their relationship.

- **Be prepared for early empty nest syndrome.** Closed rehearsals are one of the hardest parts of parenting a working child actor. It's a bit like the first day of kindergarten.

Children leave for work early in the day and don't return home until quite late in the evening. There is no parental involvement during this time even regarding schooling. It's important to listen carefully to your child for signs of stress and to develop trusting relationships with key members of the production such as the child wrangler or the tutors. The parents of other child actors are also good resources for charting these difficult waters.

- **Watch your pocketbook.** Your child is now working in the business world! Be prepared to learn about the tax implications of that and the record-keeping required to track expenses. Manage your per diem payment for expenses wisely. You will be busy driving to lessons, auditions, rehearsals, and performances. With proper planning, many families can cover unanticipated costs like travel.

Outsourcing

It's easy to become overwhelmed by the demands of your child's career on your life and time. If you don't have time to exercise, or to spend time with your other children, your friends, and your loved ones, consider outsourcing some of your responsibilities. You can hire someone to drive your child to auditions or acting classes. Don't forget about summer camp, where your child can have a great time while you recharge your batteries. Get help at home with shopping and cleaning. Make sure you have time for yourself and other family members as well as your young actor. I provide coaching services for parents of child actors who need help navigating the industry, its demands, and how it affects them.

Parenting a working child actor is tough, and yet most parents agree that the performing experience is the single best thing they ever did for both their child and themselves. As one mother of a young Broadway starlet put it, "Despite all the downfalls, the joy of seeing my child on stage makes it all worth it. It is a once in a lifetime experience I would never trade."

 These life lessons are for you, not your child! When Mom and Dad are healthy, the kids are healthy, too.

- When your child becomes an actor, your ability to manage stress and disappointment are crucial.

- Encourage positive and honest communication in your family.

- Safeguard your relationships with your spouse and other children. Don't make the focus of your family only on the actor.

- Ask for and accept help often. You don't have to be a superhero. Consider working with a coach or therapist when you feel overwhelmed.

- Find something you love doing and make it a part of your regular routine.

Chapter 15

The Teen Years

*Acting is the greatest answer to my loneliness that
I have found.*

—Claire Danes

An agent at Paradigm Talent Agency in New York, Ellen Gilbert, has been developing young talent for twenty-seven years. I asked her why it is often hard for child actors to get cast during their early teen years, a time that is often called "the dead zone." Gilbert shared that the years during puberty are particularly challenging because bodies and voices are changing. Movies need the child to look the same age throughout filming, which is a problem if the shooting lasts more than a few months. Many productions would rather use a young-looking adult instead of a teen to avoid the expense of on-site schooling and the stringent child labor laws. The ages of twelve through eighteen are tough ones for teens in theater as well, especially if they are taller than four eleven. Many short adult actors can play teen roles. Think of all the adults who played Peter Pan on stage.

Disney and Nickelodeon cast shows with real teens, and there are roles in other TV shows and in commercials for teens, so there are some opportunities for work during these years; it is not impossible to land parts. But it is challenging. Gilbert suggested, and I agree, that teens who are not getting cast use the time to take classes and enhance their acting skills. She said, "Do local theater, take classes, and improve your craft. If you still enjoy acting when you come out of the dead zone you can start to audition again. The ages between fourteen and seventeen can be full of opportunity."

The years during puberty are challenging for all teens. Acne, physical changes, and social pressures can be challenging. It is natural for teens to doubt themselves and feel awkward, homely, and confused. Add these natural teen challenges to the frequent rejections during auditions and a teen's desire for independence... what's a parent to do?

Clinical psychologist Dr. Nancy B. Austin of New York City said that an essential developmental milestone during adolescence is the ability to separate from parents while still maintaining a positive connection. Austin advised, "One of the main things that parents can do is to let the child know they support the child's decision to enter the world of acting, and even if not chosen for the role, the child hears that the parents are proud of her for trying. Yes, trying counts."

Austin also pointed out, "Teen years are a crucial time to develop empathy, which is based on the ability to see the other's point of view. This skill is constantly reinforced in acting. Trying out how others experience the world through acting may give your adolescent actor a head start in understanding how others may feel and why they do the things they do. When talking to your child about the disappointments that are a necessary part of the field of acting, focusing on empathy – why others behave the way they do – can be the essential healing ingredient."

Try your best to help your teen navigate the highs and lows of friendships and dating during the teen years. If you feel overwhelmed by the complications of helping them balance the demands of acting and relationships, consider consulting with a therapist or life coach.

Increase Responsibility

Gabriel Rush started acting at age ten with a touring company in *101 Dalmatians.* Since then he has appeared on Broadway in *Billy Elliot* and in the movies *Moonrise Kingdom* and *Grand Budapest Hotel*, and has been featured on several television shows. I asked Gabriel to talk about his transition from child actor through his teen years. Gabriel shared, "My parents were wonderful supporters of my acting career and still are today. I could not have made it without them. Around fifteen or sixteen I started taking more responsibility for the communication with my agent and manager. Instead of my mom calling with reports on auditions, questions about costumes, or to communicate concerns, I made those calls. I also took on responsibility for my schedule and finding ways to fit in my studies with my acting. Taking on this responsibility gave me an edge when I got to college. I already knew how to communicate well and manage my time. I knew I could function in college because I learned how to be mature and act like an adult."

Here's a list of twenty-five things you can encourage your teen to do in taking more responsibility for their career and transitioning from child to adult. Discuss this list with your teen. They might have other ideas as well.

Before leaving for an audition:

1. Prepare, organize, and copy headshots and resumes.
2. Measure your height and jot it down.
3. Scan a headshot, resume, state work permit, and/or trust account paperwork for distribution by email.
4. Create a demo reel and maintain it with updated footage if necessary.
5. Create an audition record using your smart phone or iPad; include contact information and requirements for each audition.

6. Take a full body picture as a photo record of clothing, hairstyle, and makeup.

7. Take a picture of the odometer to capture starting mileage.

8. Take pictures of your sides so you can practice them on the go.

Traveling to or from an audition:

9. Capture personal thoughts, ideas, reflections, and new goals.

10. Write down feedback from the casting director.

11. Update contact information for new professional contacts.

12. Invite the kids you talked to in the waiting area to be friends on your Facebook page.

13. Write thank you notes.

14. Take pictures of receipts for meals, tolls, lodging, and other expenses (don't forget the odometer at the end of your trip) and fill out an expense record from the receipts captured.

15. Use an app to improve memorization.

16. Do your homework for school. (It's important!)

While waiting:

17. Check online sources for audition notices (weekly).

18. Find and sign up for new classes and workshops.

19. Maintain the family calendar and your personal calendar: enter rehearsals, classes, and auditions; watch for family conflicts and propose solutions.

20. Research new monologue and song material.

21. Make a list of new plays and books to read.

With your family:

22. Review and update audition materials.

23. Set priorities regarding family commitments and conflicts; adjust your calendar as necessary.

24. Review and set goals for training and audition opportunities; discuss how they impact the schedule and budget.

25. Budget for classes, auditions, clothing, and accessories; compare to actual expenses.

Teach time-management techniques and help them learn to prioritize. For example, your teen might be invited to a pool party, need to prepare for an upcoming audition, and have a paper to write for school. Instead of telling them what to do, ask open-ended questions like:

- Which of these things are the most important to you?
- Why are they important?
- Can you figure out a way to do what you want to do and still do what you need to do?

Your teen is learning, so don't expect perfection. Each time they make a choice about how they want to spend their free time, do your best to coach them through the decision-making process instead of just telling them what to do. When things go awry, talk about what happened so they can learn from the situation. It's easy just to say "Because I told you so," but fight that urge and take advantage of each teachable moment, knowing that you are providing valuable life lessons.

Physical Changes

Adolescence can bring growth spurts, acne, frizzy hair, and crooked teeth. Do your best to help your teen make peace with these changes. Remind them that everyone goes through an awkward adolescent period. Have them do a search for photos of other actors to see how they changed during the teen years. Old yearbook photos can provide some laughs, so share some of your high school memories and funny looks.

Provide support in helping them look their best. If acne is a problem, visit a dermatologist. Encourage healthy eating and plenty of exercise. Help them select clothing that feels right, and advise girls about appropriate levels of cosmetics.

Braces

If your child needs glasses or braces, consult with professionals about the least intrusive options. Braces can be a challenge for young actors. I spoke with family orthodontist Dr. Gerald Gardner to get his advice on this one: "The best time to be evaluated for orthodontic treatment is between the ages of nine and eleven. One thing to remember is some children at the age of nine can have a mouth of an eleven-year-old, and some eleven-year-olds can have a mouth of a nine-year-old. A trained orthodontist can evaluate the child to decide the best time to start treatment."

If your child is working or auditioning regularly at this age, consult with your orthodontist and see if holding off a few years is acceptable. That would bring your child to the awkward teen years when work tends to slow down anyway.

Many parents think using a clear tooth-alignment system such as Invisalign® is an easy fix, but Gardner believes that Invisalign has limitations and generally does not produce the same results as traditional braces. Although you can remove them for auditions, they might not correct the teeth. After spending all of that money, your child could wind up needing metal braces after all.

Parents also think they can easily get braces removed for an audition or job. "Think about this one carefully before acting on it," said Gardner. "Removal of braces can add cost when braces have to be replaced. It can also extend the treatment time." However, it might be worth it if it means getting a big role, so talk it over with your family and agent or manager.

There are some instances in which children can work with braces. Occasionally children with braces are needed for an on-camera television commercial, film, or TV role. Voice-overs are not a problem for a child with braces unless the equipment in the mouth creates a speech problem. Many children working on stage opt for clear braces since they can't be seen by the audience.

Braces are a regular part of life for many children and teens; just one of many things to consider as you and your child plan a show-biz career. Plan wisely and don't hesitate to discuss this with your agent or manager, but don't let it discourage you either. Your child is growing up, and with a little luck and hard work they will have many years ahead to land some fabulous roles and shine on stage – all with beautifully straight teeth.

When Roles Dry Up

Talk with your child about timing and remind them that the teen years are challenging for everyone. It's the perfect time to:

- **Take classes to learn technique.** As your teen becomes a more mature performer, they will be required to master skills that are beyond their natural ability. Enroll them in an ongoing acting class with a teacher you both like and trust. Teen actors need training, especially in technique.

- **Expand their range of skills.** Suggest that your teen train in new areas such as a new style of dance, martial arts, vocal training, or even a sport like fencing. Training in new areas builds confidence. This is also a good time to learn new dialects. Dialects are part of the basic training of every good actor. Suggest taking time well before opportunity knocks to learn a few of the more popular dialects such as Standard British, Cockney, Irish, Australian, Southern, and Brooklyn. Dialects are not only about pronunciation but also about cadence, phrasing, inflection, and pitch. It is important to work with a trained coach on mastering the nuances of each dialect.

- **Don't stop acting.** Encourage your teen to act for the joy of it in school plays, community theater, or student films. Playing roles, whether they are paid or not, expands acting skills.

- **Read plays.** Teens who regularly read plays literally explode with ideas when they read new scripts. And, as a bonus, they can find unique monologues and scenes to explore in class and to present at auditions. Below are some of my favorite plays for teen performers to read. Some are new and others classics. They are all well written, good literature, and have been successfully produced.

  Brighton Beach Memoirs by Neil Simon
  The Loman Family Picnic by Donald Margulies
  Really Really by Paul Downs Colaizzo
  A Raisin in the Sun by Lorraine Hansberry
  Leaves by Lucy Caldwell
  Be Aggressive by Annie Weisman
  Picnic by William Inge
  Ascension Day by Timothy Mason
  Our Town by Thornton Wilder
  Speech and Debate by Stephen Karam
  The Member of the Wedding by Carson McCullers
  Women and Wallace by Jonathan Marc Sherman
  The Diary of Anne Frank by Frances Goodrich and Albert Hackett
  John Lennon and Me by Cherie Bennett
  Tigers Be Still by Kim Rosenstock
  From Up Here by Liz Flahive

  And don't forget to encourage your teen to go the theater and watch classic films. Watching good acting is an excellent way to learn.

- **Become more well-rounded.** There is more to your child than performing other people's work. The best performers are interesting people first, and casting directors pick up on that right away. A person with diverse interests who is curious and invests time in learning new subjects or acquiring new skills comes across as vital, intriguing, and attractive. Encourage your teen to develop their own distinct combination of interests outside of the performing arts, and it will help them as a performer.

Dropped by Your Rep

Unfortunately, teens who are not getting work may be dropped by their agents or managers. This can seem like a tragedy. If this happens to your teen, console them and let them discuss their feelings. Then have them get into action. Have them talk with the rep to find out why they were dropped. It could be for one of these reasons:

- Physical characteristics like height or an outdated look. One of my clients was dropped by her agent and came to me for a consultation. I immediately advised her to cut her hair before seeking new representation. It was down to her knees and made her completely unmarketable.

- Lack of training. It could be that your child needs additional skills in cold-reading, acting, or vocal quality. Have them consult with an acting teacher or coach to determine the specific areas in which they need to improve, and make plans to do so.

Help your adolescent have these conversations maturely and professionally. Remind them that this is a small industry, so poor behavior can come back to haunt them in the future. This is an excellent opportunity to practice having civil and productive conversations.

Once you and your teen have discovered and remedied any physical or training limitations, it is time to reassess their assets with a trusted professional. Get a fresh opinion of their strengths, repackage their portfolio, and shop for new representation. Agents and managers need talent. Just because your child's agent is now unwilling to handle them doesn't mean someone else won't. What is not in vogue for one representative could be just the thing another is seeking.

It might also be time to just take a break for a while. I asked psychologist Dr. Nancy Austin about warning signs that parents should look for that signal a teen needs the support of a therapist to navigate the waters of adolescence and acting. If you observe:

- Problems with eating, sleeping, or homework
- Signs of withdrawal or anxiety
- Frequent illnesses
- Lack of interest in activities that used to be enjoyable

… encourage your teen to have fun with friends and family, exercise to reduce stress, and take downtime when they can just be a kid.

 Life Lessons = Success

- There is a time for everything, and if roles are hard to get you will have other opportunities.
- You are not a victim. Look for what you can do to grow and improve.
- Time-management skills are required in every profession.
- Each choice has costs and benefits. Learning to make good decisions means deciding which benefits are most important to you.
- To work in an adult world you must manage your emotions, even when disappointed.

Chapter 16

College and the Audition Process

There is no point at which you can say, "Well, I'm successful now. I might as well take a nap."

—Carrie Fisher

I have coached many teens who matriculated into top theater programs such as those at Carnegie Mellon University, University of Michigan, University of Miami, Emerson College, Boston University, University of Southern California, Rider University, Muhlenberg College, Ithaca College, Syracuse University, Florida State University, Boston Conservatory, New York University, and Yale.

My client Carolyn Miller started working with me when she was eight. She did many commercials, voice-over work, guest appearances on television, some movies, and lots of musical theater. Carolyn's goal was to work professionally in musical theater, so she wanted get into a top-tier college program with a strong focus on musical theater. We worked together on monologues and song selections for her college auditions. Carolyn reported that each university program had a unique audition process. She was expected to demonstrate her skill in acting, singing, and dance. Carolyn did an outstanding job and was accepted at Boston Conservatory, her top college choice.

College programs are an important place to get the training needed for success in the adult acting world. I attended Florida State University in the BFA acting program and found it incredibly valuable. I gained my foundation and basic training, which helped me transition from child actress to adult actress. Not every successful adult actor attends a college theater program, but many find them extremely useful.

If your child is interested in pursuing a degree in musical theater or acting, this chapter will give you both important information. I suggest that you read this chapter with your teen and then discuss it together. I wrote most of it directly to your teen actor, primarily because it is time for them to pilot their own future. Start with this quiz:

1. I have known that I wanted to be an actor and have been performing since:
   A. Elementary school or before
   B. Middle school
   C. High school
   D. I have very little or no acting experience.
   E. I've acted in some shows but I've taken some breaks from acting too.

2. I am mostly motivated by:
   A. Making money
   B. Performing
   C. Both
   D. Neither

3. My attitude about the business of show biz is:
   A. It is something I pay attention to, but my focus is on being the best actor I can be.
   B. It turns me off or is scary.
   C. It is really interesting; I want to learn more.
   D. I'm going to be an incredible actor. The business will take care of itself.

4. Will I want to teach acting, voice, or dance someday?
   A. Yes; it would be kind of cool to teach.
   B. No; I'm on stage or bust!
   C. Not sure. Do I have to know everything at seventeen years old?

5. Are my parents okay with my decision to study acting?
   A. No; they wonder why they're about to spend all that money on an acting degree.
   B. Yes; my parents tell me to go for it.

6. Am I an unbelievable salesperson when promoting my talent and ability?
   A. Maybe not incredible, but I can hold my own.
   B. I don't have to; people notice my talent wherever I go.
   C. You bet I am, and I don't take no for an answer!
   D. The thought of self-promotion makes me nauseous.

7. Am I consistently on the high honor roll?
   A. I nail it in the classroom and on stage.
   B. My grades are good, just not the high honor roll all the time.
   C. My grades could be better, but I'm going to apply myself in college.
   D. Grades don't matter. I'm developing my talent.

8. Do I want to go to a school where there's a lot of school spirit, and cheer for really good sports teams?
   A. I'll be the one with my face painted in school colors.
   B. No way, I only watch the Super Bowl for the commercials.
   C. It might be fun, but it's not a big consideration.

9. Do I plan to work while I go to school?
   A. Absolutely; I need the dough.
   B. Probably; I could use a little extra spending cash.
   C. Not likely; I'm concentrating entirely on school during the semester.

Scoring:

1. A=2	4. A=2	8. A=0
B=2	B=0	B=2
C=1	C=0	C=1
D=0		
E=0	5. A=0	9. A=0
	B=2	B=1
2. A=0		C=2
B=2	6. A=1	
C=1	B=0	
D=0	C=2	
	D=0	
3. A=1		
B=0	7. A=2	
C=0	B=1	
D=2	C=0	
	D=0	

Results: Thirteen or less, you're leaning toward a BA. Fourteen or greater, you're leaning toward a BFA.

Before we analyze your score, let's talk about the difference between a Bachelor of Arts degree (BA) and a Bachelor of Fine Arts degree (BFA) in broadest terms. The difference is usually in the required coursework. A BA generally requires forty to forty-five semester hours of training in a performing arts concentration, such as theater, while the BFA requires seventy to eighty semester hours. In a nutshell, this means a student in a BFA program will not have time for much else. Let's look at the quiz results to see how this will impact you.

Questions 1 through 4 are meant to help you consider your goals. Students who are deeply committed and motivated to performance above other goals, including making money, are candidates for a BFA program. The extra coursework in your major provides additional opportunity to hone your craft. However, it is almost impossible to double major in the BFA track without taking more than the typical eight semesters to graduate. That makes the BA particularly appealing to students who have wide interests and talents and/or want to double major. A double major in theater and business, for example, is ideal to prepare for a career in the business of show biz. On the other hand, students who aspire to teach in the arts often choose the BFA for its rigorous, focused training and its appeal when seeking graduate programs.

Questions 5 and 6 assess whether you have the support and personal qualities to succeed in show business. Students without solid support from their families might reach a mutual understanding by pursuing a BA in theater and another major. Family support can be important when entering an exceedingly competitive career. Fearless self-promotion doesn't hurt either. If you are not sure that you are up for the challenges and sacrifices typical of actors in the business, a BA degree that gives you extensive career options could be best for you.

The remaining questions focus on the college experience. Regardless of degree type, success in school requires a commitment to hard work and smart planning. The BFA track has more required coursework in theater, and the order in which the coursework is taken often matters. Demanding courses sometimes pile up without much scheduling flexibility. Though not impossible, it can be harder to hold a job or attend football games when in the all-consuming experience of a BFA program. Students who eat, breathe, and sleep theater should go for the BFA while those who want to do it all or have many outside demands might be happier on a BA track.

The scoring on this quiz is decidedly unscientific, but the questions are designed to give you some clarity and focus. Focus on which degree and individual programs best meet your goals, and you will end up with a wonderful college experience and a promising career.

Where to Begin

College theater programs are small and competitive. Most take only ten to sixty new students each year. It's important to research many programs to find the ones that are the best fits. I urge all my students to begin thinking about what type of school and what type of program they're interested in as early as their freshman or sophomore year in high school. Then start to work on not just your audition material, but your entire portfolio. Have you excelled in school academically? If you're applying for musical theater, is your dancing up to speed? The schools themselves are not that easy to get into academically, so grades and test scores matter!

Do a Google search to find the top-ranked programs. Many websites, including The Hollywood Reporter and The Princeton Review, do annual rankings. By the way, I offer free webinars featuring interviews with directors at some of the top colleges.

The Admission Process

The college admission process is extremely competitive, especially for prominent programs. I talked with Jean McDaniel Lickson, head of the BFA acting program at my alma mater, Florida State University, and asked her for advice on the admission process. She said:

> We are looking for more than just talent. Discipline and preparedness are also important. This is a tough business. You've got to be prepared to be economical, responsible and disciplined with your time. That's what a good actor is.
>
> We can tell a lot about someone in their interview. Work on your interview skills, be yourself, and be ready to give thoughtful answers to these questions:
>
> What are my values?
> What do I believe in?
> Am I disciplined enough to do this, because it is a hard life?

We want you to be great and your wonderful self. Show us you love what you do. Be who you are, not who you think we want you to be.

Those are wise words that I wholeheartedly agree with.

Each university has its own admission process, but most ask for a *pre-screening* video (to be received before your audition and/or interview) that showcases your talent – both acting and singing if it's a musical theater program. They are looking for natural talent and honesty, not formulaic performances.

Most ask for a video with two contrasting monologues. It is important that these monologues be carefully chosen. Usually two contemporary pieces, a drama and a comedy, are preferred. I don't recommend using dialects.

Catherine Weidner, the chair of the Department of Theater Arts at Ithaca College, shared, "We're looking for people who come through their material. I like to say that what I really look for is inner life. I look for somebody who believes inherently in the character or the message of the material. We're really looking for connection."

Jean McDaniel Lickson added, "What we're looking for is a sense of presence, really living in the moment and really listening and responding to the person you are talking to. We want to see you have a change in your monologue from the beginning to the end and can see you are starting to form a character. We don't want performers. We want real human beings as characters. That's what we are looking for and that's hard to do."

Choose monologues and songs that show contrast and are age appropriate. Acting happens when you try to get what you want, so ask yourself, "What am I doing to get what I want?" All the non-verbal communication of a character who is falling apart or falling in love gives a monologue life beyond the words. You cannot communicate all that emotion if you are simply focusing on the words.

Since monologues are such a pivotal part of the college audition process, I highly recommend that students work with their acting coaches on the selection and performance of monologues. Use these tips when considering monologues:

- **Be a smart risk-taker.** Stay away from nudity and be mindful of profanity and sexually charged material unless it is appropriate for the character and not for shock value.

- **Make real life your art.** Find monologues that easily connect to personal experiences, thoughts, and emotions that have been important in your life. Material that speaks to you in this intimate way allows you to connect to the character and demonstrate the depth of your understanding. College and high school auditions always require you to demonstrate depth, not your full range.

- **Be age-appropriate.** There are many monologues for complex, age-appropriate characters. It shows poor preparation when a teen attempts to play Blanche in *A Streetcar Named Desire* because she played that character in a high school performance. If you want to impress your professors in high school or college, do the research to find quality age-appropriate material.

- **Don't scream.** Surprise your audience with the unexpected by doing the opposite. It can be much more powerful and interesting to play a menacing character in a quiet, contained voice. Yelling can make the character seem one-dimensional, and that is an audition killer!

- **Avoid material from monologue books, which tend to be overused.** Select unique pieces that mean something to you.

- **Work with a coach who is experienced in assisting with college auditions to get the help you need in choosing material and performing it successfully.**

You might be asked to submit a video audition. The video does not need to be perfect or professionally produced. Instead it should be honest and demonstrate that you understand the material and can make choices about it. Review chapter 11 for tips on self-taping to ensure that your pre-screening video represents you well.

If the program professor is interested in you, you will be invited to audition on campus or at National Unified Auditions (Unifieds), which are held in Chicago, New York, and Los Angeles. Unifieds allow students to audition for numerous university programs in one location over the course of a few days. This saves the student time and money and also allows the university to audition a wider range of students than they might on campus. This can also be a disadvantage. One of my very strong musical theater students was sick the day of his Unified audition and was not able to perform well. For this reason, even if you do go to Unifieds, I recommend also auditioning on the campuses of the schools you most want to attend.

Each university has its own process for on-campus visits. Some do a half-day program, others a full day, and some campuses conduct a full weekend of tours, workshops, and auditions.

Catherine Weidner revealed, "People think they have to come in the room and perform for us. But actually what we're looking for is people who can come in the room, and be present, and be relaxed and focused, and enjoy themselves. Because it's not a career or a business where you want to be miserable or nervous, not that being nervous is a bad thing, but we really want people that are alive and healthy, and have a terrific attitude towards the way that they work."

It's Not Just the Performance

Your attitude and personality will be evaluated in addition to your performance. Weidner told this story:

> I was standing in the hallway in New York last year. There was a girl singing in the audition room. It was incredible. There were two other girls sitting in the hallway on the

bench, waiting. One girl, the one about to go in, just had this terrified look on her face like "There's no way I'm going to be able to compete with that." The girl next to her tapped her on the knee and said, "You're going to be just fine." I thought, "That's what it's all about. It's not about whether we take her over you. It's whether we think that what you have is right for our program." I was so impressed with her attitude. When she walked in the room, I just thought, "I like her already."

Kaitlin Hopkins echoed that sentiment:

At Texas State, we're not just looking for talented artists. We're looking for good humans who also have an exceptional work ethic and are a joy to have in the room. We read every single essay. Those essays really matter because they contribute a great deal to why we call people back. We really want to know what you think your strengths and weaknesses are, not just as a person, but as an artist. Then we're looking at your grades, and your test scores and all of that contributes. We're interested in developing artists into strong collaborators and consummate professionals. That's very much the process here. Because frankly, it's an industry where there's a lot of very talented people, so why is this young woman, or young man, going to be cast in that show over another? A lot of it has to do with your reputation, your integrity, and who you are as a person.

Lauren Lane is the head of the BFA program at Texas State. I asked her to tell me about an audition that blew her away. "One young man was extremely shy. In his day-to-day life, he would characterize himself very confidently as an introvert. His work was extraordinarily present and honest. It wasn't like he was using a lot of technique. He had done technical work on the text, etc. But he was able to achieve an open simplicity that was magical. Then he discussed very openly and honestly, 'I am an introvert. I spend a lot of time at my grandmother's farm.' He was a cool kid. He was just honest about who he was. It was evident he was somebody I wanted to work with."

Finally, know that there is no perfect audition. Kaitlin Hopkins offers this advice: "I don't want perfect. I want messy. You can put together this perfect package, and if you can do it the same way twenty times in a row, that is only impressive if it is still alive and in the moment. I want you to have a point of view in the world of the character. I want to see who you are."

If all this seems overwhelming, know that help is available. There are coaches who can help you with all the aspects of the college application and audition process. You don't have to do it alone.

 Life Lessons = Success

- Grades matter, even during freshman year.
- It is necessary to plan ahead to reach a big goal.
- No one wants to work with an ill-tempered diva or bad boy. Who you are is as important as your talent.
- Train in all areas of theater, even if you don't feel like a great singer or dancer. You don't have to be a rock star to develop competence in areas outside of your comfort zone.
- Writing skills are important for college essays and future career success.

Chapter 17

Moving Forward

My goal has always been not to look forward to the next thing, but to relish and celebrate the successes I have at the moment. Whether it's landing a part in a student film or having a good day in acting class, I never discredit anything.
—Dianna Agron

Now that you've learned some of the particulars of the business and read all about the life lessons your child will learn from performing, I hope that you can see many benefits awaiting your young actor. The media likes to hype the stories of child stars who struggled or crumpled under the pressure. However, in my thirty years of experience in this business, I have seen just the opposite. The vast majority of child actors I have known grew into accomplished, successful adults whether they stayed with acting or pursued another path.

Much of your child's adult success will be influenced by you and your parenting. Using the life lessons in *Parenting in the Spotlight* will help you guide your young actor through some of the challenges of being a child performer. Being a part of the acting community, whether in local productions or on a Broadway stage, brings a wealth of experiences and memories to your family.

I have one final life lesson to share with you. Developing an acting career takes time, especially if your child wants to act as an adult. As you know, I've worked with famous stars like Scarlett Johansson, Mira Sorvino, and Lacey Chabert, among many others. They started as children and invested at least ten years in their careers before they achieved stardom. There is no such thing as an overnight success.

I've also worked with many young actors who did not become household names but are successful and happy in their adult lives. Jacob Barandes started acting when he was a kindergartener. He did some commercials, a student film directed by Sara Gilbert, and a television pilot. Today Jacob has his doctorate and teaches at Harvard. He uses his acting abilities regularly. He said, "Engaging teaching is a performance art at some level because without being able to keep the interest of students, it's hard to teach them effectively. Speaking clearly and with a good rhythm, being able to convey emotion and subtlety, being able to discern how others are feeling, knowing how to construct a compelling narrative, having a well-tuned sense of humor, and knowing a little improv are crucial skills, and my background in acting has therefore been very helpful. I also teach students how to give research talks, and those especially involve serious acting skills, such as doing a good job selling oneself to an audience that might not be inclined to take one's work seriously. Acting boosts a person's charisma, which is a crucial quality to have in so many aspects of life and work."

A former student of mine, Anya Wallach, fell in love with performing when she was selected to perform during the taping of a live Nickelodeon show called *Total Panic*. At twelve she landed a role in a production of *Annie*. By age sixteen she had founded her own children's theater in Westchester County, New York. When she wasn't auditioning, Anya was directing and working in her non-profit theater. Today Anya is the executive director of the internationally renowned Random Farms Kids' Theater and is the co-author of the *Stagestruck* book series published by Sleeping Bear Press. Her experiences as a child performer led her to her career. She said, "Being a child performer helped me develop a thick skin because there's a lot of rejection involved. It also taught me about discipline and structuring my time, since you had to learn how to squeeze in homework and a social life between late night rehearsals. Since I still work in the arts, I'm also appreciative of the skills I learned while performing in musicals. The vocal, dance and acting training I got has helped me to hire artistic staff, as well as when we're casting."

Anya had some great advice for parents: "It's funny, my parents were not 'theater people,' but I think the parents of child performers could learn a lot from them. They were great at letting me lead – and they realized the difference between being a parent and being a teacher. I had plenty of directors and coaches – their role as my mom and dad was to support and encourage me. I think a lot of parents start to get really invested in wanting their child to succeed, and they start to take on the role of instructor. That often isn't a healthy dynamic for child/parent – it's really hard for a kid to be receptive to that kind of criticism or even direction from Mom or Dad."

You read about Travis Greisler in the first chapter. He told his mother, Wendy, when he was six years old, that he wanted to be a director. Travis went on to star on Broadway and in touring productions of *The Who's Tommy*, *Les Miserables*, and *Big*. Today Travis is a director, just as he predicted years ago. He told me, "I don't think I would be the kind of person I am without my childhood career. It was that growing-up experience and learning how to be a professional from such a young age that created much of my drive as an artist, and even as a person. That all came from the amount of work that I was doing as a kid."

When I asked Travis if he had any advice for parents of kids who want to perform, he said:

> My advice would be, follow your child's lead. They will always let you know how interested or not they are at any given point. Their career, this business, this industry will always be there. If they need a break, let them. When they're ready they can come back to the business. Their education, the kind of young adults they are going to turn into, is far more important than any role, any opportunity, anything that comes their way. But if they love performing, if they can't get enough of it, if the support from the industry itself keeps encouraging their work, yeah, keep going. Encourage their love of this art form, because it's an incredible thing to be a part of. I think when handled in the right way, it can make you an incredible young adult.
>
> I have a lot of incredible skill sets that were instilled in me from my parents and working so young. My father taught me from a very young age that it was important to network and keep up with people. I got to be on two national tours and therefore I saw a lot of this country and life in other cultures. The food, art, and all the new things to explore made me into the adventuresome person I am today. There is not a bad thing that I could say about my experience acting. But that is also because I was fortunate enough to have parents who kept me grounded and my priorities straight.

Travis is right. No matter what level of success your child achieves in the performing arts, the greatest gift you can give is to parent effectively. Take the life lessons in this book and use them with your budding child star and your other children. You'll be glad you did!

Glossary of Useful Industry Terms

ADR: Automated dialogue replacement, sometimes called looping or dubbing, is when the original actor re-records their dialogue and dubs over their lines for improvement in audio quality.

Agent: A person whose job it is to solicit employment and secure work for their clients as actors, directors, musicians, writers, producers, models, professional athletes, and even animals, while supporting and promoting the interests of their clients.

Blocked Trust Account: Required in California, New York, Louisiana, and New Mexico to protect 15 percent of a minor actor's earnings until adulthood. It might be referred to as a Coogan account, but that is only its legal name in California.

Booking: Getting hired for the job.

Breakdown: A description of a performance project that includes a storyline synopsis and descriptions of all the characters/roles in the script. It also commonly includes the names of the people involved in the project, such as the directors, casting directors, and producers, as well as an estimated start date and location of the production.

CSA: Casting Society of America, the organization for casting directors in film, television, theater, and new media.

Callback: A second or additional audition after an initial interview or audition.

Casting director: The producer's representative responsible for selecting performers in a film, play, or other production.

Cold-read: Reading aloud a scene or sides in an audition with little or no rehearsal.

Commission: Percentage of a performer's earnings that is paid to an agent or manager for their services.

Coogan account: Named after child actor Jackie Coogan, this is a blocked trust account required by law for all performers under the age of eighteen in the state of California, designed to safeguard 15 percent of their gross earnings until they enter adulthood.

Copy: A commercial or voice-over script.

Demo reel (or reel): A short audio or video used to market oneself for audition purposes.

Dialect: A regional accent that an actor uses to make a role more believable.

Emancipated minor: A person under the age of eighteen who has been given the legal status of an adult by a judge.

Equity: Actors' Equity Association (AEA) – the union governing live theatrical productions.

Extras: Actors hired for background non-speaking roles.

First refusal: A non-contractual courtesy requesting that a performer notify a casting director before accepting a booking for another job on the same day in order to give the casting director the option of "refusing" to let the performer take the job because they are expected to be on the casting director's job.

Headshot or 8 x 10: An 8″ x 10″ photograph used by actors for casting consideration.

Hold (on hold): A contractual obligation for a performer to be available for work.

Improvisation: Spontaneous dialogue that helps actors find reality within themselves while performing without a script.

Industrial film (industrials): Often an educational film, tape, or DVD that is not broadcast.

Local hire: An actor hired locally for a production (usually TV or film) where it is being shot, which eliminates costs for travel, housing, and per diem.

Looping: Recording background sound post-production to add voices to all the background actors. Looping adds quality to the production!

Manager: A talent manager guides and cultivates a career. They counsel, advise, and provide career direction and guidance. They have fewer clients than an agent, which enables them to provide personalized attention. Managers take anywhere from 10 to 20 percent commission, and usually sign a client to a three-year contract.

Monologue: A speech presented by a single character used mostly for auditions for stage productions or representation.

Must join: If it has been thirty days since your first SAG-AFTRA booking, you "must join" the union before your next union job.

Off book: Saying lines from memory without using the script.

Open call: An interview or audition open to anyone.

Pilot: The initial television show that introduces the characters and situations for a potential series.

Pilot season: The time of year (usually January through April) when most television pilots are cast.

Portfolio: Headshots, resume, and sometimes reel.

Principal: A performer with lines or with significant importance to the storyline.

Producer: The person responsible for making day-to-day decisions regarding a play, TV show, film, or any broadcast production.

Read-through: Usually the first rehearsal when the actors sit and read through the script with the director.

Residual: The fee paid to a performer for subsequent showings of a commercial, film, or TV program.

Resume: A list of credits, training, and skills. Your resume should be attached to a headshot.

Right-to-work states: States in the US that do not require agreements between unions and performers, meaning you don't have to join a union to get a job.

SAG-AFTRA: Screen Actors Guild – Actors Federation of Television and Radio Artists, the labor union representing actors in film, television, radio, and video games; announcers and newspersons; singers and recording artists; performers in commercials in all forms of media; and actors working as stunt persons and specialty acts.

Scale: The minimum payment for services under union contracts.

Scale + 10: The minimum payment plus an extra 10 percent to cover the agent's commission.

Series regular: An actor in a main role in a TV series who appears in most if not all of the episodes.

Sides: Pages or scenes from a script used by performers selected for auditions that highlight a specific character.

Sitcoms, multi-camera: The classic sitcom filming method with a laugh track and three cameras in fixed locations. They are generally filmed before live audiences. Examples: *Seinfeld*, *Friends*, and *Big Bang Theory*.

Sitcoms, single camera: A more contemporary filming approach with no laugh track and cameras that move around for a variety of shots. They are filmed without an audience present. Examples: *Modern Family*, *Silicon Valley*, and *Arrested Development*.

Slate: In on-camera auditions, the performer's introduction of their name, age (if under eighteen), and sometimes height, hometown, and agency.

Standby: In theater, a performer who is not in the show but will take over for an actor who needs to miss a show or leave mid-performance.

Stage manager: The person who oversees the technical aspects of a theatrical or in-studio production.

Studio teacher: As defined under California labor law, a teacher with dual California certification – elementary education and high school secondary – who is responsible to the Department of Labor to advocate on set for the "health, safety, and morals" of the minors in their charge and to teach them when school is in session. "Studio teacher" has incorrectly become synonymous with "onset tutor," the latter being an individual with a teaching degree who does not have any other responsibility than to teach.

Submission: An actor's or agent's suggestion of an actor to a casting director for a role in an individual production.

Swing: In theater, a cast member who understudies several chorus and/or dancing roles.

Taft-Hartley: A federal statute that allows a thirty-day grace period after an actor's first day of employment before requiring them to join the union.

Triple threat: An actor who can sing, dance, and act skillfully and equally well, usually referring to performers in musical theater.

Typecasting: Casting performers based on their "look."

U-5 (under five): Literally a role with under five lines.

Understudy: A performer who is hired to replace an actor who is sick or unable to perform. They are usually already a cast member in the show.

Voice-over (or VO): An off-camera or off-stage voice heard without the appearance of the performer.

Work permit: Issued by a state or local agency, a required legal document allowing a minor under the age of eighteen to work on creative or artistic projects.

Wrap: Finishing a production.

Acknowledgments

This book would not be possible without the help and encouragement of many people. I am extremely grateful for the tremendous team of support and friendship on this journey.

I wouldn't be where I am today without two remarkable women, Jean Fox and Adrienne Albert, who gave me my start in this industry. They were like mothers to me when I began thirty years ago, and today remain my dear friends. Their talent management company, Fox Albert Management, helped launch many illustrious careers, and their guidance and mentorship taught me how to be honest, loving, and humble.

Thank you to my life coach and mentor, Marion Franklin, for partnering with me to find my authenticity as I rediscovered myself. Marion's efforts led me to my amazing editor, Lynne Klippel, whose belief and faith in me helped me find my true voice in *Parenting in the Spotlight*. Lynne and her team are consummate professionals and I know we will work together for many years to come.

Thanks to *Backstage* magazine, which posts my articles online and in print and helps me carry the message to young performers and their families nationwide.

Thank you to Alan Simon for teaching me how to become a successful entrepreneur and for your generous contributions and insight as an expert in educating young performers.

Thank you to Ray Rosenblum, whose belief in me gave me the fortitude to write this book. I will be forever grateful for your contributions, words, inspiration, and ideas.

Thank you to Sally Gaglini for legal counsel and collaborative friendship.

Thank you to Sheryl Berk and Lisa Sharkey for your generous advice.

Thank you to Carol Moritz, who taught me I can have anything my heart desires just by asking.

Thanks to my LOL group and best girlfriends ever: Lauren Z., Debbi, Sharon, Shelley, Linda, Susan, Kim, Wendy, Leslie, Marjorie, Ann, Randi S., Randi C., Nancy, Sue, Laurie, and Peggy, who all believe I am superwoman and give me the fuel to soar. A special thanks to Debbi, Kim, and Wendy for reading my drafts and brainstorming at all hours of the night. Thank you to my best friend, Lizzie, who believes in me even when I have doubts.

A big ol' kiss to my canine best friend, Bailey, who sat at my feet and gave me comfort, making the writing process enjoyable.

Thank you to Kevin Johnson, my marketing manager and social media guru, who masterfully handles my online presence. Thanks also to Jennifer Butler, my assistant, who keeps my life running smoothly so I can do this work.

A special thank you to Susan Annar and Lisa Albano for editing, brainstorming, and contributing great ideas.

Thanks for the expert medical advice and contributions from Doctors Jay Berk, Nancy Austin, and Lisa Sussman.

Thank you to my wonderful colleagues in the business: agents, managers, casting directors, directors, and teachers, including Bob Marks, Badiene Magaziner, Monica Robinson, Julia Mendelsohn, Renae Baker, Travis Greisler, and Jazelle Foster, for your collaboration and contributions.

Thank you to my Aunt Lee, who has always believed I could achieve anything, and more.

Thank you to my daughter Julia, for your unending support. You are my audience and voice of reason as I edit, practice, and rehearse what I want to say, and most important, how I say it. Even though I strive for perfection, you remind me it's okay to be average.

Thank you to my parents, Don and Sandy Dunayer, who have supported my creative endeavors from the time I was a little girl. Your faith, love, and belief in me taught me, "Yes I can!"

Thank you to all of my clients and colleagues who shared their stories and experiences for inspiration to young performers and their families.

To my teachers, Burt Reynolds, Charles Nelson Reilly, and Wynn Handman: You taught me that acting is hard, to tell the truth, and if you say you're going to do something… *do it!*

I am so lucky to work in an industry that brings me so much joy. Thank you to the many clients, students, and parents whom I have taught, guided, and mentored. Thank you for trusting me with your kids and teaching me how to be a better teacher and human. You make me love what I do!!

About the Author

Denise Simon is recommended by New York's top agents, managers, and casting directors for her ability to coach young actors *without* their looking coached.

Denise has a gift for speaking the language of young actors and communicating in a way that instills confidence and builds skill sets. Her classes and industry workshops attract both established and emerging talent. She has coached *hundreds* of children and young adults, privately and on set, who appear regularly on Broadway and in TV and film.

A veteran of the industry as an actress, teacher, director, casting director, and personal talent manager, Denise has expertise in coaching performers in the craft not only through private lessons but also through weekly classes, group workshops, summer productions, industry showcases, and college teleseminars. Denise provides private consulting to guide young actors and their parents through the challenges inherent in show business. She works with high school students on their college auditions and guides them through the performing-arts college admission process.

As a certified life coach, Denise works with clients of all ages to help them find balance and satisfaction in their lives. Her life-coaching skills give her insight into clients' needs. For parents of young performers, this means guiding them to be more effective in their roles as advocates for their children. Denise's training helps her understand that in the process of pursuing an acting career, children can develop their character and abilities in ways that impact them positively throughout their lives. With her assistance, children learn meaningful life lessons that they take with them to whatever careers they choose later on.

Denise is an expert columnist at Backstage.com, is a member of the New York SAG-AFTRA Young Performers Committee, and has led seminars for Actors' Equity Association and SAG-AFTRA. She has also worked with corporate firms leading acting and improvisational training for their employees.

For ten years Denise was an associate with Fox Albert Management, one of the leading talent management companies in New York, where she worked with clients such as Scarlett Johansson, Academy Award winner Mira Sorvino, Lacey Chabert, and Judy Reyes. A graduate of Florida State University with a BFA Degree in Acting, Denise studied acting with renowned teachers including Wynn Handman, Burt Reynolds, and Charles Nelson Reilly.

Denise has a long history of working with young actors. She created the youth division at Total Theater Lab in New York City and founded Out of Sync, a teenage comedy improvisational troupe. Denise worked at several youth theater camps including Stagedoor Manor and Long Lake Arts Camp. She cast the award-winning independent film *No Letting Go*, directed by Jonathan Bucari. Her directing credits include *A Midsummer Night's Dream, The 25th Annual Putnam County Spelling Bee, Working, You're a Good Man Charlie Brown,* and *Into the Woods.* She was the on-set coach for the award-winning television show *Teen Kids News* and for Fox Television's *The Following*.

Denise lives in New York where she enjoys attending the theater, cycling, hiking, and the rich culture of Manhattan.

Index

D

E

F

G

H

I

K

44699614R00119

Made in the USA
Middletown, DE
14 June 2017

Every new generation of children is enthralled by the famous stories in our Well-Loved Tales series. Younger ones love to have the stories read to them. Older children enjoy the exciting stories in an easy-to-read text.

LADYBIRD BOOKS, INC.
Lewiston, Maine 04240 U.S.A.
© LADYBIRD BOOKS LTD MCMLXXI
Loughborough, Leicestershire, England

Printed in England

Goldilocks
and the
Three Bears

retold for easy reading
by VERA SOUTHGATE

illustrated by ERIC WINTER

Ladybird Books

Once upon a time there were three bears who lived in a little house in a forest. Father Bear was a very big bear. Mother Bear was a medium-sized bear. Baby Bear was just a tiny, little bear.

One morning, Mother Bear cooked some porridge for breakfast. She put it into three bowls. There was a very big bowl for Father Bear, a medium-sized bowl for Mother Bear, and a tiny, little bowl for Baby Bear.

The porridge was very hot, so the three bears went for a walk in the forest while it cooled.

At the edge of the forest, in another little house, there lived a little girl. Her golden hair was so long that she could sit on it. She was called Goldilocks.

On that very same morning, before breakfast, Goldilocks went for a walk in the forest.

Soon Goldilocks came to the little house where the three bears lived. The door was open, and she peeked inside. No one was there, so she walked in.

Goldilocks saw the three bowls of porridge and the three spoons on the table. The porridge smelled good, and Goldilocks was hungry because she had not had her breakfast.

Goldilocks picked up the very big spoon and tasted the porridge in the very big bowl. It was too hot!

Then she picked up the medium-sized spoon and tasted the porridge in the medium-sized bowl. It was lumpy!

Then she picked up the tiny, little spoon and tasted the porridge in the tiny, little bowl. It was just right!

Soon she had eaten it all up!

Then Goldilocks saw three chairs—
a very big chair, a medium-sized
chair, and a tiny, little chair.

She sat in the very big chair. It was
too high!

She sat in the medium-sized chair.
It was too hard!

Then she sat in the tiny, little
chair. It was just right!

But Goldilocks was too heavy for the tiny, little chair. The seat began to crack, and then it broke.

Oh, dear! Goldilocks had broken the tiny, little chair, and she was very sorry.

Next Goldilocks went into the bedroom. There she saw three beds—a very big bed, a medium-sized bed, and a tiny, little bed.

She was tired and wanted to go to sleep.

So Goldilocks climbed up onto the very big bed. It was too hard!

Then she climbed up onto the medium-sized bed. It was too soft!

Then Goldilocks lay down on the tiny, little bed. It was just right! Soon she was fast asleep.

In a little while, the three bears came home for breakfast.

Father Bear looked at his very big porridge bowl and said in a very loud voice, "Who has been eating *my* porridge?"

Mother Bear looked at her medium-sized porridge bowl and said in a medium-sized voice, "Who has been eating *my* porridge?"

Baby Bear looked at his tiny, little porridge bowl and said in a tiny, little voice, "Who has been eating *my* porridge—and eaten it all up?"

Next Father Bear looked at his very big chair. "Who has been sitting in *my* chair?" he asked in a very loud voice.

Then Mother Bear looked at her medium-sized chair. "Who has been sitting in *my* chair?" she asked in a medium-sized voice.